Reachi...

Reclaiming His Passion

WHAT HUSBANDS NEED

Judy
Carden

D1167855

Kregel
Publications

To Bob—my beloved.
After all these years, loving you
and being loved by you
still delights my heart with breathless wonder.

What Husbands Need: Reaching His Heart and Reclaiming His Passion
© 2006 by Judy Carden

Published by Kregel Publications, a division of Kregel, Inc., P.O. Box 2607, Grand Rapids, MI 49501.

The stories, interviews, and personal excerpts in this book are, to the best of my knowledge, true events. Because of the sensitive nature of this book, however, many names have been changed to protect the privacy of the contributors and the sacredness of the sacrament of marriage.

Unless otherwise indicated, Scripture quotations are taken from the *New American Standard Bible*. Copyright © 1960, 1962, 1963, 1968, 1971, 1972, 1973, 1975, 1977, 1995 by The Lockman Foundation.

Scripture quotations marked NIV are from the *Holy Bible, New International Version*®. Copyright © 1973, 1978, 1984 by International Bible Society. Used by permission of Zondervan Publishing House.

Scripture quotations marked NLT are taken from the *Holy Bible, New Living Translation*, copyright © 1996. Used by permission of Tyndale House Publishers, Inc., Wheaton, Illinois 60189. All rights reserved.

"If Only I Had Known You" © 1974 Nancy Spiegelberg, is used by permission of the poet. Nancy's poetry can be accessed at www.godthoughts.com.

Library of Congress Cataloging-in-Publication Data
Carden, Judy.
   What husbands need : reaching his heart and reclaiming his passion / by Judy Carden.
      p. cm.
   ISBN 0-8254-2407-0
   1. Marriage. 2. Marriage—Religious aspects—Christianity. 3. Husbands—Psychology. 4. Wives—Conduct of life. 5. Love. I. Title.
HQ734.C279 2006
248.8'435--dc22   2005036168

Printed in the United States of America

06 07 08 09 10 / 5 4 3 2 1

Contents

Acknowledgments

A NOT-SO-FUNNY THING happened during the final months of writing this book: my family, along with families of countless other Florida communities like ours, experienced three unexpected and life-altering events. Their names were hurricanes Charley, Frances, and Jeanne. In our predominantly rural area alone, we experienced an unprecedented three hurricanes in six weeks.

As cleanup and rebuilding efforts continue, the loss of life, property, and of daily routines leaves us longing for a normal day. Yet as I write from the haven of an unscathed chapel here in Winter Haven, I am reminded of the goodness of God's people. It is because of the extraordinary efforts of "ordinary" people that you are able to turn to this page today. These are the unsung heroes who worked (and continue to work) long hours, under less-than-ideal conditions. To those power and telephone linemen, debris removal teams, arborists, roofers, contractors, government officials, and insurance adjusters, I am forever grateful for your service.

Bless the hearts and hands of the others who helped birth this book. Matt Jacobson, faithful friend and agent, thank you for your vigorous insistence on the highest measure of performance, particularly when writing words based on God's timeless truths.

To Dennis Hillman, Kregel publisher, my enormous gratitude for the gracious manner in which you responded to news of the storms. Each hurricane added weeks to the completion of this book.

Janyre and Moriah chipped, chiseled, and polished the manuscript to the level of professionalism worthy of bearing the Kregel name. Thank you.

David Leitzke kept my computer functioning, gallantly bailing me out with each new crash and crisis.

To Aubrey, Suzi, LeAnn, Millie, Chrissy, Amy, Joni, Connie, Suz, Kelly, Janette, Shay, and Judy, thank you for reading and catching those "bloopers" my own eyes missed. Peggy—with the help of your mother, Christine—you are the treasure that allows me to write *and* manage our home. Without you, mayhem would ensue. A dear friend, Amy R., offered her services as a personal assistant. Then in the eleventh hour, energized by a considerable consumption of sugar, Carolyn, Connie, and Lauren joined me for an evening of giggling, eating, and editing.

Danny and Ryan, my precious sons, remember always that you are gentlemen and scholars, and I shall dance at your weddings!

But the many husbands, with their willingness to share those seldom spoken longings about love and marriage, are the heart and soul of this book. Gentlemen, your transparencies are agents of the heart that act as compelling catalysts for change. I am indebted to you.

To Bob, my beloved: your character and constancy breathes energy into my soul. The many sacrifices you made over this past year merely reflect the man you are. Because of your gentle but determined encouragement, especially in the aftermath of such disaster, I am able to complete this labor of love.

And now I'm going to settle in for a long winter's nap.

ad majorem Dei gloria

Introduction

For where your treasure is, there your heart will be also.

—Matthew 6:21

As LITTLE GIRLS, most of us were captivated by the mystery and magic of romance. It was scripted in our hearts long before we were born. Remember how we dreamed of becoming a bride? We saw the role we were created to play as beautiful, magical, and worthy. And on our wedding day, the future was filled with the promise of bright tomorrows.

What we didn't know is that, with the passing of time and familiarity of daily life, a marriage can lose its magic. Busyness takes over. Too little time together causes stress, which results in a breakdown in communication, which results in dwindling romance. Conflicts creep in. Tenderness fades. The relationship becomes routine and our husband's needs are a burden. An undeniable sadness settles over the marriage and our husband seems distant. Then, from somewhere deep within, we feel a flicker of that nearly forgotten romance and remember there is no miracle greater than the power of love. And we want it back.

This book is a tale of true love. It is an epic romance, based upon the very first love story, detailing God's unmistakable and purposeful design of a husband and wife. In reading this book, He is offering you the chance to write the rest of your love story. *What Husbands Need* is a journey of faith, commitment, and love. One where your tender heart and teachable spirit will greatly affect the rest of your story. Its message is this: if you desire the joy of a *truly* great marriage, try focusing on the needs of your husband. *What Husbands Need* is not just another book pointing out what wives are doing wrong. This book *shows* us how to live out God's best—as women and wives—and reap the blessings He wishes to bestow on us!

7

Marriage is the first human relationship to appear in the Bible, emphasizing its obvious importance to God. Thus, beautifully illustrated in Genesis, we see that marriage is His gift to Adam and Eve. God's creative work was not complete until He made Eve. He had a better plan: "It is not good for the man to be alone; I will make him a helper suitable for him" (Gen. 2:18).

Unlike Adam, whom God created from particles of dust and breathed life into, God *fashioned* a woman from the rib of Adam's flesh to be his helpmate. "The LORD God fashioned into a woman the rib which He had taken from the man" (Gen. 2:22).

Notice that Scripture says He "fashioned" her. Imagine how much thought God must have given to the molding and shaping—physically, emotionally, and spiritually—of man's counterpart! Paying meticulous attention to every detail of His masterpiece, He understood the magnitude of *this* creation, for, without her, man was incomplete. After all, *woman, the crown of all creation*, was the rest of the love story.

Could it be that, in our contemporary world, we have become misguided and so we overlook the power of our authentic design? Do we compete with our husband rather than complete him? And have we forgotten not only how to be a helpmate but *how much* hard work love requires?

The reality is, even our intact families' lives are fractured. We women are exhausted as life in our fast-paced world sweeps by with barely a rustle. A large mortgage holds us hostage, making it necessary for many of us to work outside the home. Yet stay-at-home mothers, volunteers for nonprofit organizations, and empty nesters also admit to being overcommitted. While in pursuit of purpose and personal fulfillment, I fear we have left something far more precious behind: our husbands.

Indeed, our worldly ambitions, child-rearing responsibilities, and extracurricular activities have left us little energy for the man we married. Have we been too busy to hear the longings of our husband's heart?

Consequently, our husbands are lonelier than ever. They are so hungry for our love they have strayed from the bonds of marriage in heartbreaking numbers, looking for intimacy and affection from any woman willing to give it. Sadly, we have been looking for purpose in all the wrong places. The irony is there is no place where a woman has more power and purpose than in the home with her husband.

We are technologically superior to the generations before us. We have oceans of information at our fingertips. Recent surveys indicate women are more intelligent, more ambitious, and more independent than ever before. Yet even now, at the top of the heap, so to speak, you may find yourself wondering: Can we be as happy as we once were? What does my husband want? What does he need from me? What really makes him happy? Can I win back the heart of the husband I unwittingly left behind?

Whether you've been married for fifty years or are a disillusioned newlywed, if you find yourself seeking answers to these questions, you have chosen the right book. Born from the timeless truths of Scripture, *What Husbands Need* embarks upon a journey of discovery—a journey to discover what God put into your husband's heart.

In preparation for this book, I interviewed dozens of men who were willing to be candid about what they yearn for from their wives. Their transparency will amaze you, as will the depth of their disclosures. Their tender responses to my online questionnaires touched uncharted areas of my own heart—areas I never knew existed! I kept a much-needed box of tissues close at hand.

For the first time in my life, I understood the core of a man's heart. Certain discoveries lanced my heart, for this sacred glimpse into men's hearts revealed to me those many times I have failed my own husband.

To be honest, I frequently struggled with these revelations. Eventually, though, reaching for faith rather than fear, I applied the truths I discovered to building an even richer relationship with my husband. And I learned that, in the tale of true love, forgiveness begets forgiveness, breathing new life into love.

Today, the newness of that love in my own marriage sets my heart aflutter. And it gets better! Our husbands yearn to be with us. They yearn for us to make them a priority in our lives. Believe it or not, our husbands still covet the mystery and wonder of the relationship they experienced back in the day of our love's tender beginnings. Our husbands hunger for our love and respect. They thrive on our encouragement and praise. They long to defend our honor. They implore us to stand behind them in steadfast prayer. They want to be strong for us, praying for, and protecting us.

Sisters in Christ, it is time to turn our hearts back toward home. Time to look upon our greatest treasure, our husbands, with fresh and tender eyes. It's time to reclaim our marriages. And while I am not suggesting that we quit our jobs, abandon our children, and sever all ties within the community, I am suggesting it is time to tighten our focus. Time to listen to the longings of our husband's heart. Time to take that wisdom and impress it on our hearts. Time to love our husbands the way God has called us to love them.

God desires for you the very best marriage: a marriage that truly reflects the relationship spoken of in His Book. Thus, my book begins with my heartfelt prayer that these words speak to your soul so that you might discover for yourself the longings of your husband's heart.

By everyday standards, I am simply a small-town woman, wife, and mother. I have neither a theological nor a counseling degree. And I am still learning of my husband's needs. But with each passing day, even as I embrace these principles, I watch with wonder while God writes an extraordinary, revised edition of the story of my marriage.

It has been written that reading books changes lives. Perhaps you are asking, *Will this book help my marriage? It seems to be in a state of disrepair.* Or maybe you think your relationship is strong but could benefit from a little more magic. Either way, I wholeheartedly encourage you to embark on this journey. You have nothing to lose and everything to gain. I invite you to watch with wonder as you apply these principles to your marriage.

Be prepared to change—and get ready *for* change—as God rewrites the second half of your love story....

My command is this: Love each other as I have loved you.

—John 15:12 NIV

The rain came down, the streams rose, and the winds blew and beat against that house; yet it did not fall, because it had its foundation on the rock.

—Matthew 7:25 NIV

When we bestow on our husband honor, admiration, and encouragement, we can behold as he reaches for the prize of his highest calling . . . becoming the leader of the home.

—Millie Farthing,
speaker and retreat leader

Chapter 1

Respect

The Deepest Measure of Devotion

IN THE BEGINNING, were the words: promises exchanged during a dreamy candlelit wedding ceremony. But in the beginning, when we were crazy in love with our husband, the pledge to love and respect him was a painless promise to make. After all, he was our knight in shining armor, the man of our dreams and, by far, the easiest guy in the world to respect. Right?

But somewhere along the way, somewhere between our marriage vows and mortgage payments, somewhere between the magical and the mundane, we learned there is more to the words, "I promise to love and honor you," than we had originally thought. Much, much more . . .

When Respect Is Lost

It wasn't until Gray and Carol were airborne, forty thousand feet above the daily demands and routine of running a household, that an awkward silence finally fell over them.

"Gray," Carol began in an attempt to break the silence between them, "I'm so glad we're getting away together."

Gray, nestled in seat 3B, nodded, and then returned to the book he was reading. Engrossed, it was obvious he didn't wish to talk. Carol thought it somewhat strange, considering that Gray wasn't much of a reader.

Bewildered and defeated, Carol abandoned her attempt to make conversation. Giant tears splashed onto the pages of the magazine lying across her lap. She wondered if the thud of her sinking heart was audible to her other seatmate as it dropped somewhere between disappointment and despair.

When was the last time Gray was in the mood for laughter, love, or a long conversation? What caused this "hollowness" in our marriage? What made him withdraw? Each thought brought about a new wave of heartache. She missed the days before financial success snatched happiness out from under them. The days when Gray had been the leader of their family.

Describing Gray as a combination of John Wayne, the Lone Ranger, and King David, she emphasized that, "Like John Wayne, he is a warrior. He even has the swagger that suggests: mess with my wife or kids and you're going down! A man's man, he is respected by most men, intimidating to others, and admired by women. Like the Lone Ranger, he single-handedly tackles any challenges presented to him." Most important though, according to Carol, is that Gray, much like King David, has *always* had a heart after God.

Spiritually and emotionally, they had been blessed beyond measure. Amazingly, Gray's business grew 400 percent over a three-year period. Then prosperity, lurking like a thief in the night, snuck into their home and seized her husband's heart. Taking his eyes off God, his humble heart turned haughty and hard. It was on the flight to Scottsdale that Carol could no longer deny the inexplicable sadness that had infiltrated their ten-year-old marriage.

It is frightening how easy it becomes, when blinded by anger or pain, to stumble over our husband when he has fallen as a result of his failures. Especially when we get a really good "mad" brewing. The thought of lifting him in love and prayer is difficult, if not, at least in our mind, humanly impossible.

Falling into the above category, Carol's respect for the man she once respected more than any man alive was all but nonexistent. Skeptically, she was convinced the only way she would regain respect for him would be if it was divinely resurrected. Little did she know that was precisely God's plan.

When God Grabs Hold of Your Heart

The next morning, Gray attended the first of several conference meetings. Resting poolside at the resort, Carol thumbed through travel destinations she thought might be of interest to them. They had agreed that neither had the heart to participate in the "dog and pony show" that preceded these conferences. They had two days—and a rental car—to call their own.

Suddenly, Gray's voice interrupted her thoughts. "Have any ideas how you'd like to spend the next two days?"

Carol did, but had no idea why. You know that feeling you get when your heart is "nudged" and "thumped" with such persistence it's impossible to ignore? It makes no sense and you feel silly following through with it, yet not following through is not an option. So off they drove.

Visiting the Grand Canyon the next day was God's reminder to Gray and Carol of His magnificence and majesty. The beauty of the canyon left them breathless, knowing only God could create such a masterpiece from hard and jagged stone.

The following morning the "nudging" persisted while packing the car. Looking at the map, they noticed that the city of Sedona was on their return route to Scottsdale. A particular point of interest was the Sedona Chapel built on the bluffs of the famed red rock formations. Carol read no further. They were headed toward the bluffs, and three hours later they arrived.

Have you ever unknowingly wandered onto holy ground? Defenses disappear. False bravados fade. Well-constructed walls come tumbling down. And somehow you sense you are resting in His holiness.

That's what happened to Gray and Carol. The instant they entered the vestibule of the tiny chapel, in front of God and strangers they began weeping. Carol had only seen her husband cry once when his father passed away. After all, everyone knows John Wayne types don't cry. Fortunately, God sees things differently. He seized hold of their hearts and had no intention of releasing them until they allowed Him to create beauty from their jagged hearts of stone.

Making no attempt at false composure, they turned and walked downstairs to a gift shop. Neither spoke, but both purchased a small memento for each other and returned to the chapel.

How often has God tried to get you to voluntarily drop to your knees in prayer, particularly for your husband? But mixed emotions of the flesh prevented you from doing so. For months God had asked Carol to drop to her knees, but she had been more concerned

> *Remember how eager you once were in your pledge to love and respect your husband. Recall also that there was no clause containing the phrase "only when perfect and deserving of our respect."*

that Gray do so. After all, *he* was the one with the problem. He was the one who'd made money his God. Not her. In her mind she was the loving wife.

"Finally God brought me to my knees, but, because I had not done so willingly, the result of my actions proved painful," Carol admitted. "Apparently," she continued, "this was not only about Gray's failures—the ones I'd been pointing out for months. This was about mine as well."

In that chapel, strangers must have watched them with embarrassed curiosity, yet Carol only recalls both of them dropping to their knees, facing each other on the step of the altar. And they, without previous notion, renewed their wedding vows.

> *Take his strong points — those very characteristics that originally drew you to him — and actually implement them in your marriage. For example, if your husband has terrific money-management skills and your family's finances need a revised strategy, encourage him to devise a financial plan that provides both short-term sensibility and long-range security.*

But God was not yet finished with Carol's heart. Still kneeling, hands interlocked, Gray whispered, "I took my eyes off God. Power and prosperity became my gods. You and the children fell to a distant second. I've been selfish, shortsighted, and undeserving of your respect. For that I am sorry. But before God and all that is holy in this chapel, I love you and know where I went wrong. The book I was reading on the plane is *Go the Distance* by John Trent. He asks men if we're equipped to cross the finish line faithful to the promises we made. Boy, has God jerked me by the neck. I give you my word, I *will* be a man who goes the distance. But I need your love and respect to do it."

In an instant, the hollowness that echoed throughout their marriage of late made sense. Suddenly, Carol remembered when she had withdrawn her respect from Gray. Several months earlier, she questioned (and judged rather harshly) his capability and worth as a businessman, husband, and father. *That* was the day the tide shifted in their marriage, and that was the day he instinctively withdrew.

Through their tears, they asked forgiveness for the ways they had failed each other. They asked for the chance to renew their once-tender love and to see Christ in the face of the other, as God had intended.

Reflecting on Our Own Relationship

Surely you can recall the days when your own romance was bright and brand-new. *Your* love was close to perfect. You tenderly lavished honor on your husband. A mere glimpse of him made your heart beat faster. His whispered words took your breath away. He was witty, wise, and brilliant.

You blinked and, without warning, you were buried beneath a burden of bills, babies, and business deadlines. Soon, the mundane overshadowed the magical. And you discovered your knight in shining armor suddenly seemed rusty and dull.

> *Completely resist the temptation to point out your husband's shortcomings. (He already knows them!)*

Now his way of doing things causes you to poke and pounce on him—from the way he changes the baby's diaper to how he disciplines the older children to how he fails to pick up his dirty socks. Then you *really* hit him where it hurts: you second-guess his business decisions. You question his capabilities. Honor is withdrawn. An unspoken war is waged.

Sadly, we sometimes become so preoccupied with our own issues, we don't even notice when our husband has silently retreated from us. Perhaps remaining benignly polite, he stops sharing with us. We tell ourselves that life has just gotten busy. The truth is, he doesn't feel "safe" with us anymore. It is then, for fear of being further rejected and disrespected by us, he withdraws his affections. A once-vibrant house slowly turns into a lifeless, if functional, dormitory.

How easily hollowness can replace happiness. Oh, the irony. We wives *wanted* these real men and *married* these real men, then forgot they *are* real men! Which of course means they are not perfect. But we react to their imperfections by withholding honor. Or we launch a verbal assault before they know they're even standing in the line of fire. And we wonder why a swagger turns into a stagger?

What happened to the vow to love and honor our husbands all the days of our lives, in good times and in bad? *Yes, well, that was romance, this is reality*, we may attempt to justify. At last check, there was no rider clause releasing us from that promise just because we don't particularly *approve* of our husband's attitude. Think about how you feel when you are being judged. Don't you automatically retreat— protecting yourself from the wrath of judgment? Your husband is no different. In fact, to a man, our failure to love and respect him is like dropping a weapon of mass destruction on him.

In most instances within a healthy marriage, our failure to respect our husband is not because we don't love him, though that's exactly what it says to him. Perhaps we've permitted ourselves to grow careless. Do we allow disappointment to develop into disparaging remarks? Let's be honest, when our eyes become critical and our tongue turns sharp, there isn't a man alive who stands a chance of survival. Hence we learn a painful lesson, where praise and admiration enrich love, criticism and condemnation erode it.

> *Keep all disagreements in private where they belong.*

How We Interpret Respect

Could our struggle with marital respect be the consequence of taking our eyes off God and the beautiful love He ordains in marriage? In the echoes of he-did-she-did, he-said-she-said scenarios, have we simply forgotten how to champion our husband's causes? Have the sounds of life in the fast lane drowned out the cries of our husband's heart?

Perhaps we should back up a bit and ask ourselves, *Just how does the concept of respecting our husband resonate?*

When a group of us wives were asked recently if we "almost always" showed honor and respect toward our husbands, most answered with an emphatic "Yes!"

"Take caution then," counseled our wise friend, "because most of you would be surprised to note that your body language and tone of voice might suggest otherwise."

My own emphatic "yes" was quickly canceled out by some not-so-pleasant truths. Hadn't I (even as I worked on this very book!) been cross and short-tempered with my husband? I shuddered recalling the times my responses to his questions were marked with scowls, heavy sighs, or even rolling eyes. It's just as Jesus warns us in Matthew 12:34, the mouth speaks out of that which fills the heart.

Our Heart Reveals the Real Story

When we attempt to respect our husband with our own imperfect, sometimes wounded or angry heart, it's no wonder we bristle! And, as women in this society, is it any wonder that the feminist notion that respect equates with weakness, subservience, and subjugation has affected us? Pay close attention to the next four or five articles you read in popular women's periodicals. How is the woman who is thoughtful, nurturing, and honoring of her husband portrayed?

It is when we look into our "God heart" that we are able to see our husband with the value, attributes, and potential our Father sees in him. Even looking at our husband through the hearts of others can reinforce how wonderful he is. When I visit our family-owned insurance agency, at times, I am reminded of my husband's many wonderful qualities when I see the amount of respect and appreciation his staff shows him. Sometimes when I visit I am complacent and take him for granted. At other times,

> *Lavish praise and affirmation upon your husband.*

I'm annoyed with him because of something he has or has not done. But by the time I walk out the door, I "see" him through the staff's eyes and am reminded of his value as a man.

Romance is easy to espouse when love is fresh and new. The success of a lasting love, however, is dependent on the indwelling of the Holy Spirit in our heart. With His indwelling, we are better equipped to see goodness in our husband and speak blessings to him even when our flesh doesn't particularly feel like it.

Does making a conscious choice to treat our husband with honor make us a doormat? Within the context of healthy boundaries, absolutely not! Consider the book of Proverbs and Solomon's desire to impart wisdom for godly living. What a timeless reminder that "The heart of the wise instructs his mouth and adds persuasiveness to his lips. Pleasant words are a honeycomb, sweet to the soul and healing to the bones" (Prov. 16:23–24). Imagine the power of speaking blessings to your husband!

Interestingly, the word *proverb* comes from a Hebrew word that means to govern or rule. Thus, our simply having knowledge of honor and respect is not enough. It is when we take the knowledge from the Word and live out what we learn, that it becomes the wisdom that governs or rules our heart. What governs your heart?

What Husbands Need

Just for a moment, listen. If we listen with our "God heart" rather than our hurried, wounded, or indignant heart, perhaps we will hear our husband whispering the longings of his heart to us:

"I need for you to respect me. It makes me feel important. Please, fortify me with frequent words of encouragement and praise. Don't beat me down with a steady stream of criticism and correction."

"Though I am far from perfect, please love me the way you did the day you said you would love me forever."

"With your respect—with you believing in me—I can be the man God calls me to be. Without it, I am only half that man."

————

Respecting our husband is a choice, albeit a difficult one at times. It is a choice that can take an ordinary marriage and turn it into something sweet and new. Respect can heal the broken parts of our husband's spirit and transform the depth of his very being.

Love him with the same tender heart with which you first fell in love with him! Write notes of encouragement and tuck them in his briefcase, backpack, or lunch box.

We Are Who We Believe We Are

Respecting a man can cause a transformation so dramatic it rewrites a family's heritage for generations to come. Tom Nguyen understands the power of respect. One moment of undeserved honor completely changed his life.

Tom Nguyen was one of thousands in his small South Vietnamese village who survived the war, fall of Saigon, and heinous cruelties inflicted by the North Vietnamese soldiers. The little boy who loved the Lord with his whole heart had become a drug addict and thief. Disgraced, his family sent him to live with a distant relative. As the train pulled into the village he would call home, Tom was sure this was where his life would end.

After stepping off the train, he walked aimlessly along the tracks. Soon, a small boy approached him and, smiling, looked up at Tom and said, "Good morning, sir!"

"No one had ever called me 'sir,' a term of extreme honor in Vietnam," explained Tom. "I had only been called terrible names— names I deserved. Yet when this little boy called me 'sir,' I knew I must live up to the standard of 'sir.' That was the day my life changed. After that, I made every choice in my life as a man of honor."

Today Tom Nguyen, central Florida husband and father of four, is a beloved leader in business, ministry, and community. He is living proof that we become precisely who we believe ourselves to be.

In God's Strength, Not Our Own

It is not by chance that in John 15:12 God *commands*, rather than *suggests*, that we love each other as He has loved us. He knew long before He finished flinging the stars across the sky how murky modern-day mass media would make His original design of respect. He knew how fickle and fainthearted we would be—after all He created us! He knew our feelings would fluctuate and our emotions would vacillate and that if we "gave" love only when the mood struck, marriages would be doomed before they began.

Fortunately for us, with God we have a forever love—a love given freely, with no strings attached. His love is not given only when "that loving feeling" happens to strike His fancy or when He thinks we deserve it. Nor is it given only when all business matters in heaven are A-OK and there are no areas of concern entered in His Palm Pilot.

As modern women in a contemporary world, are we listening to Him? Or are we guilty of gathering feel-good truths that are easier to live by? Just as Paul warned in his second letter to Timothy, "The time will come when they will not endure sound doctrine; but wanting to have their ears tickled, they will accumulate for themselves teachers in accordance to their own desires, and will turn away their ears from the truth and will turn aside to myths" (2 Tim. 4:3–4).

Ironically, God answered the desire of our hearts: He blessed us with those "real" men for which we prayed. The "real" men we couldn't live without. And now we come running to Him crying, "Hey, God, this marriage thing with these 'real' men is a lot harder than we thought. Help!"

Perhaps God wants us to see that He created each of our "real" men with a precarious, but precious, place in their hearts for us. A place well disguised under the false bravado and swagger of John Wayne prototypes. But know this: To honor our husband is the purest form of love. And it makes all the difference in both the man and the marriage.

Respect, simply translated, is to hold in high regard and esteem and is at the top of your husband's list of needs. How will you respond to your husband's need for honor and respect? Will you love him with your "God heart" rather than your own?

Reflection

Feelings fluctuate. Emotions vacillate. But when we love our husband—truly love our husband as God asks of us—we can transform the depth of his being.

My flesh and my heart may fail,
But God is the strength of my heart and my portion forever.

—Psalm 73:26

Lord,
I crawled
across the barrenness
to You
with my empty cup
uncertain
in asking
any small drop
Of refreshment.

If only
I had known You
better
I'd have come
Running
With a bucket.

—Nancy Spiegelberg

Chapter 2

Prayer

The Priceless Promise of Love

ONCE IN A lifetime, we may be blessed with a love of fairy-tale proportions. Theirs seemed such an extraordinary story with picture-perfect promise—Gracie and Michael, their hands and hearts entwined, pledging that when the dark clouds, deafening thunder, and drenching rains of difficulty finally fell, those storms of life would not drown out their hopes and dreams.

Then one day, and long before they had anticipated, dark clouds threatened their marriage. Gracie remembers, "as though it were yesterday," the day the two of them sat in the wingback chairs in their family room. With a trace of sadness still lingering in her voice, she wonders how two college sweethearts with so much promise for the "perfect" union could end up shipwrecked in a storm of such fury.

In the Eye of the Storm

"It felt as though we were clinging to separate pieces of driftwood and floating farther apart from each other, each caught in different and very dangerous currents," Gracie shared in a hushed tone.

"Through the storm, I still loved my husband very much. But disappointment and despair had infiltrated our daily life. For the first time in years, I felt my faith faltering. So much so, I wasn't sure how or if God could even resurrect our relationship. And heaven knows I had spent nearly every waking moment trying to get this godly man to see the error of his ways."

Gracie's heart was broken, her spirit crushed. The wonderful man she had married only seven years before was doing battle with his soul. Though his law firm had grown substantially over the years, he was no longer happy practicing law. His external façade was arrogance, but internally he felt frustrated, frightened, and not sure of where to turn. He knew Gracie had grown accustomed to the lifestyle they had worked hard to attain, and he didn't want to jeopardize that. After awhile, he began to shut Gracie out, thinking he was protecting her from his private turmoil. She in turn grew fearful, which only fueled her fear of what she didn't know. He was at war with his own heart, and Gracie couldn't help but think the worst.

As they sat there on that bleak January afternoon, each slumped in opposite chairs, Gracie cried out to Michael, "I have tried everything I know to reach you. I have tried talking lovingly to you, only to have you dismiss me with insincere promises that you would change your ways. Then, in my frustration, I have regrettably spoken harshly to you, hoping to change you back into the man you used to be. You, in turn, made matters worse by responding in anger. Your anger has completely crushed me. You are a stranger to me. I don't know how to reach you, and I feel like our dreams for our marriage have died. I've lost the man I love.

Pray specific Scriptures over your husband, according to his needs. Ask him what he'd like you to pray for! If he is unsure and you can't discern his needs, pray in general terms. God knows what your husband needs most. Be faithful. Don't fall out of step with your prayer commitment just because you happen to miss a day of prayer.

"It grieves me to say this, but I give up," Gracie conceded, as tears splashed down her already-strained face. And in her final moment of exasperation, she cried out, "If you won't listen to me, maybe you'll listen to . . . to . . . God! Even so, I'm not so sure if God could repair the mess you've made of things!"

A Tender Heart Is a Teachable Spirit

The moment the words left her mouth, Gracie was startled to sense God whispering to her broken spirit: Yes, I will repair the mess you children have made of things. I'll take your marriage and transform it into a masterpiece—the way I intended it to be. But are you willing to listen? For your heart has hardened. Will you allow Me to create in you a pure and clean heart? Will you recommit your marriage to Me? And will you see Michael as I do—as a favored son?

Her response, though more out of desperation than dedication, was without hesitation: Yes, Father, yes, yes, yes.

In retrospect, Gracie now knows that dark winter's day was the birthing of "part two" of their marriage. That was the day she began praying—really praying—for Michael, seeing him as God's favored son. She realized that in her overzealousness to improve her husband, praying that God would change him, she conveniently "forgot" about her own flaws. Her heart had hardened. She had forgotten to trust God and had been too busy alerting God to her husband's failures to be in a true state of prayer or communion with Him. She realized that before Michael could reach his full potential as the leader in their home, she first must grow in her fundamental role as a praying wife.

In her book *Choices*, Mary Farrar talks about giving our husband the best of our self, so that he may become the man God has called him to be. Quoting Corrie Ten Boom she writes, "Never be afraid to trust an unknown future to a known God."

That's exactly what Gracie did. She gave her best to God

> *Do you have a tendency to be forgetful? With all that we have to remember, if prayer is not yet a natural part of your day, why not use a reminder? One idea is to tie a ribbon to a small bell, perhaps using your husband's favorite color for the ribbon. Hang it somewhere accessible (from the rearview mirror is one suggestion). Each time the bell jingles, you are reminded to pray for your husband.*

and her husband by recommitting her bankrupt heart and spiritually withered soul to God. Only then was she in a place to ask for God's best for her husband, His favored son.

Marriage Is Not for the Faint of Heart

Can you remember a time in your marriage when you wondered if you had made a major mistake in your choice of a partner, or you wondered if you had grossly overestimated your love story and, even worse, the character of your husband? Think back to a time when you felt that your husband's performance fell far short of your expectations, or when, somewhere along the way, your beautiful love story took a detour and you weren't sure you even *liked* your husband any longer.

You may be reading this book with a heavy heart. Your spirit is crushed. Those once-soft glances are now frightened, empty stares. Perhaps privately, you are praying for either a painless parting (which doesn't exist) or a marriage miracle.

If you are looking for a painless parting, you should look elsewhere. But if you are in need of marriage "mercies," or even if you are in a "sweet place" in your marriage, please read on.

> *Do you have an accountability group or prayer partner you meet with on a regular basis? This is a wonderful way to keep accountable in praying for your husband. Remember though, share only those prayer needs or situations that your husband would be comfortable in sharing. And have an understanding that whatever is shared in confidence remains in confidence!*

It is true, men battle for their souls every day. The pressures they face are phenomenal. Secular success is equated with how high they climb the corporate ladder and how handsomely they are compensated for those efforts. Their struggles filter into family life, often without them even realizing it. Without vigilant prayer, clear communication, and a time of accountability with others, it's easy to see how the daily battle of a man's soul can quickly escalate, infiltrating the marriage and family. Prayer is vital, one young husband learned, as he faced his greatest career challenge.

The Difference Prayer Makes

"It was during my time as a new insurance agent with a nationally recognized company that I dealt with one of the greatest career challenges in my life. I knew my wife was praying for me. Her prayer, however, was not that I have great success, nor was it that I overcome the challenges I faced. It was only after being informed I would no longer be an agent for their company that I learned what Alesa's specific prayer for me had been. Only after, I began truly seeking the face of God, as a result of what the world would surely see as a failure. During this 'gut-check time' when I was forced to see what kind of man I was, and looking at all I had worked for and lost, I realized I hadn't really lost anything at all.

"Looking back," he continued, "I saw I had never really given God a chance. I was trying to do it all myself. My wife's prayer through the painful ordeal was not that I climb the corporate ladder, rather that I would grow closer to God. For I was not created to grab onto the next brass ring but to worship my God and King. Seems simple enough, yet when you think of the verse, 'Seek ye first the kingdom of God, and all these things will be added unto you,' it brings to light that we *are* to worship Him first, and all these things will be added. And I believe that means *all* things.

"I'm so thankful," he concluded, "that I am married to a true woman of God. Alesa's prayer was a selfless prayer of great discernment. She knew what was best for not only me but for our family as well. Today I work for a small, but successful insurance agency. The owner is a Christian, and we have the privilege of integrating God into every phase of the business. Because of my wife's commitment to prayer, I am a man blessed. I am a man who, most definitely, has grown closer to God."

When Your Heart Grows Faint

As you read this, you may not even be sure *how* to pray for your husband. Perhaps you are stumbling through the dark night of your relationship. You may feel angry, fearful, and emotionally exhausted because your husband is not living up to his end of the bargain. You may even feel spiritually inept.

I have felt, at one time or another, all of the above. But I have learned that uncertainty, sorrow, anger, and exhaustion do little to improve a situation. Prayer, on the other hand, will improve any situation, no matter how desperate. Growing in our

> *If you're not already doing so, begin praying with your husband. There is nothing more precious than entwining your hearts and souls in prayer. God will bless you, your husband, and your marriage!*

prayer commitment for our husband and concentrating on *our* faithfulness make us more keenly aware of God's desire to shower His faithful with blessings. If you have ever wondered if God hears your prayers and petitions, keep a prayer journal. His responses to your prayers and petitions will astound you. He is faithful!

But there are times when discouragement and desperation grip our hearts. At such times, before we can pray for our husbands, we first need to pray a heartfelt prayer for ourselves:

> *Hear my cry, O God;*
> *Give heed to my prayer.*
> *From the end of the earth I call to You when my heart is faint;*
> *Lead me to the rock that is higher than I.*
>
> —Psalm 61:1–2

When we pray, we, like David, can know that God *does* hear our cries.

> *He brought me up out of the pit of destruction, out of the miry clay,*
> *And He set my feet upon a rock making my footsteps firm.*
> *He put a new song in my mouth, a song of praise to our God.*
>
> —Psalm 40:2–3

Many times during our family's most chaotic season of kids, careers, and multiple commitments, it was those Scripture verses and others that lifted my feet out of the "miry clay." Only then was God able to show me that my husband was, in fact, His favored son. Seeing our husband as His favored son equips us with the faithfulness and persistence we need to become and remain a praying wife in all circumstances—not just when he remembers to pick up his dirty laundry, or sends us flowers, or takes the kids to the park on Saturday so we can shop, or remembers to buy tickets to our favorite symphony performance the day they go on sale.

Prayer Is Our Responsibility

Author and speaker Evelyn Christenson understands that it is often easier to pray *about* our mates than it is to pray *for* them. "Praying for spouses," she advised a group of women, "has nothing to do with rights, how we are treated, or what the other person may be doing. It is our responsibility, no matter the circumstances."

We need to be in the spirit of prayer at all times, so that prayer becomes part of our relationship with the Lord rather than a ritual.

We pray for our husband because we love him and *want* to lift all that he is and does to the throne of God.

Like a number of the men interviewed, my own husband did battle with his soul when faced with financial success in a relatively short time. Because his character had always been as steady as the seasons, his struggle blindsided me. At first I wasn't even sure how to pray. I believed the ultimate success of my prayers hinged on my feelings for him. And, quite honestly, I wasn't in the mood to pray for the man who had crushed my spirit. But an extraordinary thing happened when I began seeing him—and praying for him—as a favored son of God.

It is a good thing I began to do so, for Bob was fighting for his soul and losing ground. Taking his eyes off God for even a brief time caused him to question the truths in which he had been so firmly rooted. I wasn't capable of fixing him—not that he wanted my kind of "help." Finger pointing and hand wringing, I have learned, are not the most effective agents for change. Prayer is. When I began to pray, and traded fear for faith, I drew solace and strength from Romans 8:28, which says, "And we know that God causes all things to work together for good to those who love God, to those who are called according to His purpose."

> *For further insight and instruction into becoming a more effective praying wife, read Stormie Omartian's* The Power of a Praying Wife *(Eugene, Ore.: Harvest House, 1997).*

Through this time, I learned to love Bob enough to listen when he asks me to pray for him as well as when he doesn't ask. Sometimes when our husbands experience times of spiritual battle, they may not even recognize that they are in a battle. At such times, we need to listen closely to their silence and pray. (Listening may mean less sleep on a night when you are already bleary eyed.) While we may expect to hear a clear and unmistakable cry for help, they may be too spiritually battered and bruised to manage anything more than a whimper.

Running to the Lord

I find great solace in knowing that even though my flesh and heart will sometimes fail Bob in times of trouble, God's perfect strength and heart will not. Now when I beseech the Lord on behalf of my beloved, I no longer crawl to Him with hand outstretched holding an empty cup. I run to Him with a bucket!

Anne, a beautiful Bible study leader, provides a wonderful example of "running to God with a bucket." If ever there is a husband blanketed in prayer, it is her husband, Steve. Anne suggested that we women take a favorite psalm—I use Psalm 1—and substitute the applicable names or pronouns with the words, "His favored son, _____ [name]." For example:

"How blessed is His favored son, Bob, who does not walk in the counsel of the wicked, nor stand in the path of sinners, nor sit in the seat of scoffers! But Bob's delight is in the law of the LORD, and in His law Bob meditates day and night. His favored son, Bob, will be like a tree firmly planted by streams of water, which yields its fruit in its season and its leaf does not wither; and in whatever God's favored son, Bob, does, he prospers."

Will you accept the honor of praying for your husband, the Father's favored son? Will you listen to his battle cries—the whimpering, whispering pleas of your spiritually wounded husband?

You can give your husband no more precious gift than the gift of praying for him. Won't you join me in running to the Lord in prayer?

Reflection

Prayer is the most powerful love language in the world. There is no more precious gift you can give your husband.

Understanding is a fountain of life to those who have it.

—Proverbs 16:22 NIV

Men are like rubber bands. When they pull away, they can stretch only so far before they come springing back.

—John Gray

Chapter 3

The Gift of Breathing Room

THIS IS A tale of two wives, Hannah and April. Each loves her husband dearly. Each is blessed with a family, live in the same neighborhood, and enjoy similar lifestyles. Each has her husband's best interests at heart. Each wants her husband to be the best he can be. Hannah witnesses her husband's continued growth, and their family reaps the blessings of his confidence and commitment to family. Indeed, her husband is a happy man.

April, on the other hand, is not as fortunate. Her husband is distant and distressed. Clearly, he is not happy.

This tale portrays two women with equal goals and similar circumstances. Why, then, the dramatically different results?

Hannah's Story

Hannah intuitively understands her husband's need for solitude. She isn't hurt when he pulls away. She understands that he was not created to be her sole source of emotional intimacy. Hannah appreciates that her husband, Scott, is a hard worker and devoted family man. To her credit, she recognizes how time away for himself rests and energizes him. And each time Scott returns home—whether he's been gone for two hours or two days—he seems absolutely *crazy* about her and the children. If only for the spark of renewed affection, it is all the initiative she needs to grant him the gift of occasional autonomy, as freely and graciously as their lifestyle allows. Their home is warm and loving.

April's Story

A few streets away is a home that, curbside, looks similar to Hannah's home. The scene inside the home, however, portrays a different picture. Inside, April sees her husband's need for occasional autonomy as a threat to intimacy, rather than the cyclical mind-set of a typical man. After a much-coveted time of emotional intimacy, April feels loved and safe, while, like clockwork, Pete pulls away and withdraws.

Pete can't possibly maintain that level of intimacy indefinitely. It isn't natural. April unfortunately, wanting to hold on to the intimacy, grows sullen when she even senses his need for time alone. A frustrated, resentful Pete resigns himself to not even ask for time alone. The last time he ventured out on an overnight fishing trip with his brothers, April sulked for a week. He "walked on egg shells" until April got past her anger. Time away simply wasn't worth the penalty.

> *Freely giving your husband some breathing room translates into "I love you and recognize your need for time away from the demands of home and work."*

By maintaining her tight grip on Pete, April has smothered that which she desired most: intimacy! Unknowingly, she has interrupted her husband's natural cycle of pulling away only to return refreshed, rejuvenated, and ready for love.

We can probably all identify to some degree with this young wife. We may not like to admit it, but each of us has been clingy and cranky at some point. Unfortunately, there were no instruction leaflets for future relationships tucked alongside us in our baby bassinets. No early edition of the book The Rules, so we could get a head start on our understanding of this girl-guy thing. We need to learn as we go, and leave the past behind.

Good Intentions Are Not Enough

About ten years ago, Bob won a fishing trip to Canada for being one of the top Crop Insurance Agents nationwide. He'd worked tirelessly to provide excellent coverage for the nation's growers and was more than deserving of the trip. And did he ever need some R & R! Initially I was enthusiastic, sending him off with hugs, kisses, and a love letter tucked in his tackle box.

Unfortunately, we had an unexpected visitor while he was away: a hurricane. I was more than capable of storm-proofing our home and, with the help of family and friends, did so. Then the children and I moved to higher ground, staying with friends. Fortunately the storm turned, and we received only minimal damage.

Though I'm embarrassed to admit it, I had a meltdown, born from my frustration, the children's fear, and the fact that Bob was foot-loose and fancy-free during the hurricane. The reality that, with our airports closed, Bob couldn't fly home even if he wanted to, was lost on me. All I saw was that he was having fun and I was not. But, as the recipient of my melodramatic phone episode, you can bet he was glad flights were cancelled! In short, I nearly ruined the rest of his trip. My self-centeredness deterred the fullness of the blessing he deserved.

The upshot? My mother set me straight—quickly. With her forty plus years of marriage and her experience in raising four sons, I knew she meant business! Her counsel regarding a man's need for downtime conveyed to me those truths I needed to hear only once. I vowed to never again make the same mistake. Awareness is wonderful, but that in itself is not enough. It is the decision to change our behavior and to put that decision into action that nourishes great relationships. Now, the minute I sense my self-centeredness gaining a stronghold on a situation, I examine my heart and change my behavior before disaster strikes. And, even more importantly, I pray. Praying for a softened heart prevents my selfishness

Want to bless his socks off? Surprise your husband by arranging a trip you know he will enjoy. This makes a great birthday or Christmas gift. One woman planned, saved, and surprised her husband and sons with a Canadian fishing trip. They had a marvelous time and now continue the tradition each summer. She wisely uses her time at home alone to catch up on chick flicks with friends, to read, and to eat cereal for dinner when and if the mood strikes her! Her husband is one of the happiest men around, and she feels renewed as well. He now blesses her with an annual trip to spend time with sorority sisters. Though you should never give expecting to receive, remember that generosity often begets generosity.

from taking root: "Moreover, I will give you a new heart and put a new spirit within you; and I will remove the heart of stone from your flesh and give you a heart of flesh" (Ezek. 36:26).

How Breathing Room Transforms a Man

Not surprisingly, our husbands' insight into their innate need for occasional autonomy holds the key to our understanding. Listen to what these men have to say:

"My downtime—from taking time to exercise to a weekend hunting trip—is directly related to what's going on with my wife and kids. I've learned the more intense the issues with work and home, the more time I need alone. It gives me the chance to think things through, one step at a time."

> *Encourage your husband to have quiet time by respecting the one corner in the house he calls his own. Resist the urge to decorate it "just the way you like it." This is his space. It should reflect his personality and be the one place in the home he can rest his mind and heart. Even if it is only a corner of your living room, let it be his!*

"It's safe to say that, as a rule, men think in silence, while women think out loud. We process things differently. And the busier I am, the more alone time I need. It's the only way I know to process pressures of everyday life. For me it's survival."

"Clearing my head during time away from the responsibilities of home and business helps me to return in much better shape than when I left. My focus improves. I'm able to pay more attention to everyone and everything around me."

"I need free time each week. It's a good time for me to think, do some introspection, think about my goals and dreams, and also think through challenges at work and at home."

"Time alone helps me to refocus. It gives me a more positive outlook toward home, work, and life in general. It clears my mind. I'd like to thank my wife for that time and tell her it helps our relationship to become stronger."

"It rejuvenates me—like a recharge of the batteries. The result, of course, improves my attitude and level of motivation. And I want to give her time alone, as well."

Pay close attention to this next one . . .

"I've read all the books based on the 'rubber band' theory of pulling away, always snapping back with great intensity. I can't explain it any better than the authors, but I know it's true. I think it's hard for a wife to understand that part of a man. If she does 'understand,' it may be more recognition than understanding. While my wife understands there is a need for me to have times of solitude, she doesn't necessarily understand the need. But the breathing room she gives me deepens my appreciation and love for her. She welcomes my time away, if for no other reason than the romance and 'newness' the reunion adds to our marriage."

And finally . . .

"The best feeling in the world is when I walk through that door after being away on a retreat, and see my wife for the first time. Her smile lights up the room and my heart beats faster with excitement."

To Bless, or Not to Bless

By chance, are you asking yourself just how soon you can have your husband packed and out of the house for some much-needed solitude? On the other hand, granting him the gift of

> *When your husband does get away—whether for an hour or a weekend—leave him alone. He can't think, pray, relax, work out, fish, hunt, or enjoy a spectator sport if he has to take constant phone calls from his wife. Save the potty-training updates for his return or for his calls. And please, above all, unless it is a true emergency, do not call him with reports of your teenager's meltdown or a minute-by-minute chronicle of your workday!*

breathing room may mean a sacrifice on your part. Thus enters internal conflict. Perhaps he hasn't held up his end of the responsibilities lately. You're tired of struggling to get him to do anything requiring extra effort. You're a nap away from nuttiness. *It's not fair*, you might be thinking, *I'm tired too. And when was the last time he encouraged me to go away while he stayed home to do double duty?*

Perhaps you are seeing red right now. The idea that your husband needs quiet time really gets your goat. You're thinking, *Yeah, right! I work the same number of hours, have the same number of kids, do the same* amount of work around here (or more), and he *should* have a break? I *deserve* a break more than he *does!*

Ah, here's the catch: Life isn't always fair. Nor is marriage always equal. But isn't love giving of ourselves with an open heart, not keeping track of the give-take ratio? And, though the echo and emotion of our vow so long ago has faded with time, what about, "I promise to love you all the days of my life . . . ?"

Sometimes it *is* hard to give. When we're weary and can't recall *our* last blessing, giving a blessing is not a natural tendency. The very nature of our culture encourages us to, at least mentally, demand to know, "Hey, what about me?" Yet clearly that mind-set has failed us. A national divorce rate of over fifty percent substantiates that.

> *Let him tell you about his time away. Chances are he'll want to share with you, but don't forget that he is still your husband — not your girlfriend. His recapping of the event may not be as thorough as you'd like. Be interested, but don't interrogate him. Depending on the situation, he'll tell you what he feels is important and of interest.*

Choose to Give a Blessing

So where do we go from here? While this should never be the primary reason to give a blessing, have you considered that one blessing often begets another blessing? Think of it this way: How do you feel when your husband surprises you with something out of the ordinary? Say, he sends flowers, arranges a night on the town for the two of you, or even encourages you to call your sister and catch a chick flick. You can't wait to thank him with something special, can you?

But what happens when your husband is also overworked, overtired, and hasn't been as attentive to your needs as you'd like? Suddenly he tells you that he wants to go hunting with his brother for the weekend. The girls from the gym advise you to put your foot down and say no. "When's the last time *you* went away?" they ask, planting a seed of discontent in your heart. Then, thumbing through a fashion magazine, you're advised, for the umpteenth time it seems, to protect the ground you've gained in the fight for equality. The more you read, the more you're bombarded with the message that "it's all about me."

Yet if loving a spouse unselfishly is perceived as a weakness by society today, then we are looking for wisdom on all the wrong pages. Popular fads and fashions fade with time, whereas the timeless truths of Scripture do not. It should come as no coincidence that the most requested reading for contemporary wedding ceremonies comes from Paul in 1 Corinthians 13. He reminds us that to love someone we must be willing to set aside our desires and instincts. In verse 5, we read that love "does not act unbecomingly; it does not seek its own."

Just as life isn't always fair and marriage isn't always equal, the desires of a husband's heart will undoubtedly challenge wives from now until the end of time. Yet, God created man; man didn't create himself. Thus the fact that he desires occasional autonomy is more than a self-centered impulse. It's an innate need and, at times, his key to survival, given the day-to-day pressures he faces.

We are faced with two choices: We begrudgingly grant our husband breathing room. He's resentful (and rightfully so!), we're clingy, and while interrupting the natural pull-away-snap-back process, we smother the relationship. This can be a truth, albeit an ugly one. Or we lovingly bless our husband with the gift of breathing room. We bless him even when he is too weary to first bless us.

> *Remember the old adage: absence makes the heart grow fonder? It really is true. Give your beloved the opportunity to discover that he misses you. A little mystery works wonders in relationships. By allowing your husband to miss you without interruption from home, this magical result occurs: his desire and appreciation for you increase!*

We just read what that time away means to him and that he returns rejuvenated, deeply appreciative of his wife, and ready for the romance a reunion adds to marriage. First Corinthians 13:13 reminds us, "But now faith, hope, love, abide these three; but the greatest of these is love." This is a truth that does not fade with time. Which truth will you tattoo on your heart today?

Reflection

Granting your husband the gift of breathing room encourages his desire for intimacy with you to be reawakened with gusto!

My lover has gone down to his garden,
  to the beds of spices,
to browse in the gardens
  and to gather lilies.
I am my lover's and my lover is mine;
  he browses among the lilies.

—Song of Songs 6:2–3 NIV

God has given us different "glues" to keep us bonded to our
mate. Communication is one of those glues. By praying, or
holding hands, we communicate through simple acts of physi-
cal touch. But one of the best "glues" of all is intimacy with
our mate.

—Shay Roop,
marriage and family counselor

Chapter 4

Rekindling the Romance

IN THE BEGINNING, when love is new and exciting, a single kiss can turn into a tender taste of heaven. A knowing glance holds the power to transform into the burning desire for another moment of intimacy. Whispering sweet words and praises to each other, our hearts sing of the emotion that transcends all others.

When we are in love, our souls perform a most delicate dance together. When two are blended in perfect unison—in mind, body, and spirit—the melody is magical, the dance miraculous. This profound love is so powerful, we pray the music will play on forever.

Like most newlyweds, we become intoxicated from the high levels of oxytocin—nature's bonding hormone. Conversely, that same bonding hormone hides human flaws that inevitably surface once the romantic stage of marriage wanes. Our bliss blinds us to the imminent, more realistic seasons of marriage that lie ahead. Who could have imagined how unbelievably busy our lives would someday become?

A Moment of Truth

Fast-forward a few years. One night the poignant face of truth pays you a visit when your defenses are down—on a night when the lights are low, your loved ones are sleeping, and a reverent hush has settled over your home. You notice that instead of pressing your bodies together as lovers often do, you and your husband now sleep back-to-back. *Something has changed,* you admit to yourself, no longer able to dispel what you have tried for months to deny. *Has a wall formed between us? An invisible wall intimacy cannot penetrate?*

As fear streaks to your heart, you wonder: *Isn't this the man I once professed to be the perfect package of a man? Has the music died? Have we been caught, completely unaware, in a season of unguarded complacency? Or has*

43

the melody merely faded, drowned out by the daily distractions of living in our busy world?

One thirty-five-year-old husband and father of two shared about a particularly melancholy moment when realization struck and he wondered: "When did our marriage bed grow cold and lonely? Did she grow distant and I get lazy, or did I grow distant and she get lazy?"

That same husband also shared that the single most gut-wrenching day of his life was the day his wife told him she no longer loved him "the way she once had."

Understanding Intimacy

Perhaps you are tempted to skip this chapter. Honestly, you don't want to address this issue of intimacy. With thirty minutes carved out of your schedule to read this afternoon, you'd rather read something of a lighter nature. You're beat. The baby has an ear infection. Your fourth-grader has a book report due tomorrow. You have "room mother" phone calls to make and a prime piece of real estate to show in the morning. Or perhaps you and your husband are childless. You don't need another lecture on the importance of sex in marriage. Please don't turn the page. Reading this chapter could change your marriage.

> *Pray, asking God to open your eyes and heart to how you and your husband can make your marriage bed sizzle. Why settle for anything less?*

Did you know that one in six marriages ends in divorce within a year after the birth of the first child? Ever the culprit, chronic exhaustion is no aphrodisiac. No one understands just how sleep deprived one can be until after a baby is born. During that season, going to bed means sleeping . . . and nothing else. Hormonal changes wreak havoc on our systems. Breastfeeding lowers our estrogen, testosterone, and dopamine levels, causing the body to lose its desire for sex.

There are other factors for lowered libido in women. Depression, birth control, prescription medications, and even over-the-counter antihistamines can inhibit a woman's sex drive. Somewhere along the way, it's easy to lose our identity as a wife, as the woman who once found great pleasure and fulfillment in the physical relationship shared with her husband.

The births of additional children force yet another unexpected turn of events: you take a part-time job to supplement the family income. There's little time to address the nagging thought of your husband's need for intimacy. The years tumble forward. Each year brings increased busyness.

Ignoring his pleas for intimacy, the excuses you give each time you reject his advances eventually sound plausible. Are they plausible enough to "affair proof" your marriage? It is not just the physical act of sex that speaks to our husband. It is also the emotional and spiritual closeness that is experienced when husband and wife are truly one in body, mind, and spirit. Lavishing him with love and attention makes him feel wanted, needed, and appreciated. The hugging, holding, and tender words say to him, "You are wonderful. There is no one on earth as precious to me as you!" And isn't that what he *really* wants to know—that he is loved and makes you happy?

Perhaps you are not busy at all. Rather, you're disinterested. Somehow you lost interest, though you can't remember when. Or perhaps you have yet to experience a great physical element to your marriage. Whatever your story, Kevin Leman, in his book *Sheet Music,* brings up a profound point: "When sex dies within a marriage, a man loses something very important to him—the knowledge that he can please his wife physically. And a woman loses the satisfaction that she has a man who is enthralled by her beauty."

> *Educate yourself. For a better understanding of female sexuality, a recommended reading is Dr. Shay Roop's new book,* For Women Only: God's Design for Female Sexuality and Intimacy *(Chattanooga, Tenn.: AMG Publishers, 2004). Other great resources are Dr. Kevin Leman's* Sheet Music *(Wheaton, Ill.: Tyndale House, 2003); and William Cutrer and Sandra Glahn's* Sexual Intimacy in Marriage *(Grand Rapids: Kregel, 2001).*

This is not only about our awareness of our husband's needs, but about the effect the depth of our marital intimacy has on us—his wife! Think about it. What a wonderful, sweet way to speak to the feminine heart. Dr. Leman addresses one of a woman's deepest desires: to have a husband who is enthralled by her femininity. Yet, when we fail as wives to properly cultivate and nurture intimacy within our marriage, we suffer as well! This is yet another delightful perspective of God's design for intimacy. As women, it is our God-given, authentic femininity that is intended to arouse or awaken our husband's authentic masculinity. It is the very essence of who we are.

God's Design for Romance

We are cautioned that, as part of the marriage covenant, a husband and wife are not to withhold themselves from each other. "The husband must fulfill his duty to his wife, and likewise also the wife to her husband. The wife does not have authority over her own body, but the husband does; and likewise also the husband does not have authority over his own body, but the wife does" (1 Cor. 7:3–4).

God has reasons for His edict. Our God desires that we experience a mysterious and magical union, one where a husband is enthralled by his wife's beauty. This was part of His perfect design for us. An excellent example of such a union is found in Solomon's intimate expressions of love to his bride:

> *You have made my heart beat faster, my sister, my bride;*
> *You have made my heart beat faster with a single glance of your eyes,*
> *With a single strand of your necklace.*
> *How beautiful is your love, my sister, my bride!*
> *How much better is your love than wine,*
> *And the fragrance of your oils*
> *Than all kinds of spices!*
> *Your lips, my bride, drip honey;*
> *Honey and milk are under your tongue,*
> *And the fragrance of your garments is like the fragrance of Lebanon.*
>
> —Song of Solomon 4:9–11

Have we fallen prey to the world's view that to love and devote our life to our husband denotes weakness and dependence? Are we listening to the message that says men are lustful, sex-starved maniacs, never to be satisfied? Perhaps we have. Husbands are lonely. They need us and are incomplete without us.

When Other Needs Distract Us

Several years ago, I felt blessed to be writing a series of books with friends. After all, we were writing about relationships. And though it was a blessing in many ways, I hadn't bargained on just how much time would be required of me. Because I had added to and not taken anything from my schedule, the commitment caused unplanned stress in our marriage. I became an "absentee" wife.

I certainly did not set out to be an absentee wife, but in my exhaustion I allowed intimacy to tumble to the bottom of my priority list. It wasn't that I didn't love Bob. I adored him and always have. There simply weren't enough hours in the day to accomplish what I had set out to do. To miss my deadlines was unacceptable. The children's needs were obvious, and they quickly voiced their displeasure when those needs weren't met. Because Bob was less vocal, I brushed his desires aside. Sadly, I was too tired to see I was leaving my greatest treasure behind.

Bob's loneliness soon became my own. I, like him, missed the magic of our marriage bed. I missed the wonder of our love and how it felt to merge flesh to flesh. We both missed the blessing of intimacy that binds longtime lovers. It was frightening, because I wasn't sure how or if we would get it back. Fortunately, it wasn't long before I realized that time and guilt had stolen enough from us and, with great gusto, we reclaimed the gift given to us by God.

> *Make intimacy a priority. The best intentions mean nothing if not properly executed. Plan a date night at least once a week. Put the kids to bed early. Lock your bedroom door. Turn on some soft music. Take a bubble bath and slip into something sexy. Agree that all discussion of children and work is not permitted during your rendezvous.*

At times, I still struggle with the shift of focus required of me during a major deadline. Locked into a chapter, it can be difficult to focus on anyone or anything else. Sometimes I need a reminder from my longtime accountability sisters to keep the home fires burning. They care for me enough to speak the truth in love. I respect them enough to listen. But it is the beyond-all-words-intimacy I share with my beloved that reminds me of the rewards of keeping the romance alive.

If Only She Knew

Have you heard the timeless adage that a man in love would swim a shark-infested ocean for his woman? One man expressed that if he could get back even a fraction of the physical intimacy he once shared with his wife of ten years, he would be willing to do even more than swim a shark-infested ocean for her:

"I've told her this over and over," he wrote, "but she looks at me like she doesn't hear a word I'm saying. I know she loves me, but she puts my needs (and her own) behind the children's. Honestly, I'm glad for the chance to get this off my chest. This isn't a topic I'm going to bring up at our men's Bible study. I wish I knew how to break this cycle. I'm frustrated. If you asked her, my wife would even tell you we had a great love life before the kids took over. God knows I want her back. Please do not use our actual names. Just sign me as 'willing to dig an ocean bed for my bride in exchange for warmth in our marriage bed.'"

> *Give yourself permission to feel sensual. Ask yourself what intimacy "looks like." If it "looks" lackluster, replace those ho-hum, hand-me-down nightgowns with some razzle-dazzle negligees. Give your very visual husband a treat. Above all, in the bedroom be a woman and a wife. Leave your mommy image where it belongs: on the other side of that bedroom door!*

Could this be your husband beckoning you back to your marriage bed? While our individual stories vary, we are all guilty at one time or another of isolating ourselves from our husband. But though the stories differ, the results are universal: our marriage bed becomes a lonely place.

Could it be we have forgotten that the very fiber of who we are wields a mind-boggling power over our husband? Have we forgotten that his need for sex is not only a physical one? He needs to know we desire him. Showering our husband with affection, approval, and appreciation says what he needs to "hear" most from us: "I love you."

Husbands jumped at the chance to share their thoughts on intimacy. After creating an online questionnaire, it took two hours of collective courage for me to finally hit the "send" key on the keyboard. It was nearly midnight. Typically, responses trickle in after a day or two. Sometimes a week passes before receiving the first response. But not this time. Early the next morning when I opened my e-mail, two responses awaited me. By nine that morning, I received two more. By noon, four more followed. They poured in for days to come.

When a Man Loves a Woman

"Intimacy with my wife makes me feel content and at peace. It makes me feel loved but also whole. There is nothing between us. We become one—with no secrets. A sense of 'completeness' is reinforced. We are happier, more joyful, and have a freshness to our souls that doesn't happen any other way. Frankly, it makes me feel blessed!"

"Intimacy with my wife speaks of the closeness that will be shared with no other. It transcends all emotions and speaks of a sharing we will continue forever."

"Intimacy with my wife in the bedroom of my heart says that we are one—one flesh. It says this is not just a roommate/ business relationship that life sometimes imposes on us. What we have is an intimacy shared only between us. It also shows me in a tangible way that she recognizes my physical needs."

> *Set your inhibitions aside. Ask your husband what leaves him breathless in the bedroom. Listen, learn, and become an enthusiastic lover. Next, share your desires. This is truly an area where knowledge equals stunning satisfaction!*

"Intimacy is important. Very important! Because 'touch' is my love language, intimate touch is quite possibly more profound. Intimacy 'says' love, appreciation, and care."

"I love the anticipation and pleasure of intimacy with my wife. It is the one element sacred and exclusive to our marriage."

"After receiving this questionnaire, my wife and I talked long into the night about how her 'busyness' had taken priority over what once was a very satisfying marriage bed. Without going into further detail, let's just say my wife is back. Praise God, praise God, praise God! I am a happy man."

The Power of Sexual Pleasure

Sisters in Christ, it truly *is* God's desire for the bonds of our marriage to remain powerful and pleasurable. In Proverbs, Solomon emphasizes that sex is God's gift to a husband and wife and is *not* intended to be boring or dull:

> *Let your fountain be blessed,*
> *And rejoice in the wife of your youth.*
> *As a loving hind and a graceful doe,*
> *Let her breasts satisfy you at all times;*
> *Be exhilarated always with her love.*

> —Proverbs 5:18–19

Pleasure, in addition to procreation, is God's intention for sex within marriage. It is His perfect plan for our marriages that our love remain magical—that the dance of our bodies be miraculous, and that the "music" of our intimacy play on forever.

Interestingly, studies suggest that lovemaking elevates the level of the brain chemicals directly associated with sexual desire. In other words, the greatest way to increase our desire for intimacy is to engage in it. And guess what? It works!

> *Be aware of how even your earliest impressions of intimacy influence your marriage. Unhealthy views of sex, often from experiences past, can destroy what God intended to be beautiful. If such distortions threaten the sexual satisfaction of your marriage, seek wise counsel at once. With time, honesty, and patience, a healthy, loving understanding of intimacy can be restored.*

When a Husband Beckons His Bride

When God created women, He uniquely equipped us to be intuitive and nurturing, as well as sensual and sensitive. And the point cannot be emphasized enough: we possess tremendous power within our marriages. We can motivate our man to greatness, or destroy his very masculinity. That's how much power we wield as women!

Perhaps we just needed a reminder. Or perhaps we have lost our perspective. Could it be that we *misunderstood* our husband's "design" because we didn't know what the "bedroom of his heart" looked or felt like?

But now we know. The "bedroom of your husband's heart"—that place where he dreams of and longs for his bride—is a safe, sweet, and sacred spot. It is the room where the promise of sexual purity to one another is paramount. The place where praise is perpetual. The room where barriers are broken and turmoil is stilled. The place where intimacy, commitment, and oneness in Christ are treasured gifts of a true covenant marriage. Here there is no greater miracle than that of love, and the melody is magical—so magical it still nearly takes his breath away.

Fast-forward a few nights from today. The lights are low. The children are sleeping and a reverent hush has settled over your home. Your beloved beckons you, his bride. His voice, barely above a whisper, brings forth from you a nearly forgotten rush of passion. Your husband, already knowing your answer, smiles and ever so softly asks, "May I have this dance, my love?"

> *Should your spirit be willing, but your body unable to enjoy sex, by all means discuss the problem with your physician. As one woman married for twenty-five years shared: intercourse with her husband had become increasingly painful. After months of frustration and embarrassment, she consulted with her doctor only to discover she was in the early stages of menopause. A vaginal lubricant was recommended and the honeymoon resumed. Both husband and wife mourn the months lost to "plain old embarrassment."*

Reflection

The bedroom of your husband's heart is that sacred place where there is no greater miracle than that of love. Where, when we understand God's gift of intimacy in marriage, the melody of your love remains magical, the dance of your bodies miraculous, and the music plays on forever. . . .

This is my lover, this my friend.

—Song of Songs 5:16 NIV

When wives befriend, encourage, help, respect, and support their husbands, they take a huge step toward inoculating their marriages against death by broken heart.

—Patrick Morley

Chapter 5

Be His Lover and His Friend

A BRISK CHILL bit at the late-night air as Taylor opened the door to their SUV for her husband Kevin. It was nearly midnight when he and his flight crew arrived at the airport, and Taylor sensed, as Kevin placed his flight bag in the backseat, that all was not well in her pilot husband's world. It was late, both were tired, the baby was sleeping in the car seat, and she assumed whatever was wrong had to do with the stresses that go hand in hand with being a commercial airline pilot. Taylor could not have been further from the truth.

Pulling into the driveway thirty minutes later, Kevin asked Taylor the most shocking questions of her life: "Why haven't you let me become your best friend? And why don't you encourage me, listen to me, or make time for us anymore?"

Taylor, too stunned to respond, sat frozen in the driver's seat. Thoughts whirled through her head. *What in the world is he talking about? After eight years of marriage, I think I'm a great wife, excellent housekeeper, loving mother,* and even if I'm only a so-so cook, all the rest is great. At least I thought it was. Where did this come from?

> *In this wondrous cyberworld we live in, take advantage of e-mail! Drop him an occasional note to say "hi," just as you do with friends, to wish him a blessed day.*

With the baby tucked into her crib, Taylor asked her husband to clarify. His analogy is beautiful.

A Great Wingman Never Leaves His Lead

Raised in a military household, Kevin understood the ways of a fighter pilot long before he entered school. He compared friendship to the relationship between a fighter, who is the lead element, and

53

the crewman, who operates as a wingman. They are critical to each other's survival as they maneuver through combat missions. Most importantly, a wingman *never* leaves his lead. The wingman is always the "eyes" that watch over the lead element, while he concentrates on completing maneuvers of the assigned mission. Considering that air combat is serious business, both the lead and his wingman must always be prepared to fend off enemies. Teamwork is essential not only to the success of their mission, but to their very lives!

As Kevin continued to explain his profound vision of friendship, Taylor saw a look of pain on her husband's face that she had never before seen. She was so captivated by his intensity *and* his tenderness, she was ready to see the truth that, for years, she could not see: She had not been the trusted and loyal wingman she had set out to be eight years earlier. In fact, in many ways, she had treated the person she loved most in the world like a "friend of mediocrity." She had become cavalier with her lead element. Their marriage had been in trouble, and she had not even realized it! Feeling smaller than she could ever remember feeling, she plopped on the floor and, exhausted, suddenly remembered words of great comfort and strength: "But Jesus took him by the hand and lifted him to his feet, and he stood up" (Mark 9:27 NIV).

> *Write your husband a letter. Tell him why you are glad he is your friend. If, at this moment, the friendship factor in your marriage has suffered a "shift," list those qualities of your friendship that you treasured. Let him know you miss that element of your marriage and are ready and willing to revitalize the friendship you once shared!*

Taylor allowed God's love, comfort, and strength to lift her up, take her by the hand, and from that night on, *show* her how to be a great wingman to her lead element. Now, ten years later, after prayer, communication, commitment, and the wise counsel of others, Taylor is no longer cavalier with her lead element. She is willing to pray any prayer, seek God at all times, give time to her lead element, and is prepared to intercept any and all tactical interferences. Taylor has learned to be a great wingman and is grateful to Kevin for revealing to her how to be an integral part of their team.

From his perspective, Kevin would tell you that having his wife as his best friend has helped make him the "fighter pilot" he was created to be, as well as the happiest man in the world.

One wonders, when had Kevin and Taylor stopped being friends? Had the intimacy—the pouring out of their most personal thoughts to one another—come to an end? Did their souls feel that twinge of pain when they somehow knew they were no longer "mates"? Taylor admits to having had such thoughts, but she dismissed them as quickly as they surfaced. Time, she acknowledges, had been their number one enemy. Sadly, Taylor and Kevin had stopped sharing "quiet time" as kindred spirits. As happens to many of us, Taylor, buried in her busy life, forgot that her husband still sought her approval and encouragement.

A Husband's Heart

"If only wives knew how much power they have in their relationships with their husbands," offered one husband. "You know, when a wife does not fulfill her part as a lover *and* a friend, her neutral attitude becomes a negative force in the marriage. And I am not a proponent of divorce! A wife empowers her husband when she fulfills her part. It is when she withdraws her support that he begins to seek that power elsewhere. He feels emasculated. He seeks that power in other ways. And sometimes in destructive ways like pornography, adultery, or workaholism."

> *Together with your husband, pull out your Palm Pilots and daily planners. Have you allowed your quality time together to lapse? If not, that's great. Keep it up! If so, delete a few unnecessary commitments from your schedule. Designate one evening a week as "prime time" with your husband— just the two of you—away from home, the office, and the kids. Talk about your hopes and dreams the way you once did when you were dating. Enjoy a latte together at the local café. Share a banana split at the ice-cream shop. Pack a picnic dinner, curl up on a blanket, and eat in the park. Plan a getaway weekend. Show your husband you value spending time with him as his lover and his friend!*

Remember, though, this is not about blame but about understanding. Let's look at things from a more positive perspective and see how important the friendship factor of our relationship is to our husband. You'll be surprised to read what our husbands have to say:

> *Make home a veritable resting place for your husband's weary heart, a sanctuary that soothes his soul, a place of peace, and a haven where love wraps her tender arms around him and welcomes him back to the place where he belongs. Let him truly feel, "There's no place like home."*

"The term soul mate or best friend does not adequately convey the closeness I feel with my wife. She is truly a part of me—we are one. Her loyalty, grace, and unselfishness leave me wondering why God blessed me with her! I am forever grateful to Him. My only wish is that I could be to her what she is to me. I am still trying."

"You ask why it is important to a man that his wife be his soul mate? A man *has* to have somebody that he can be real with. We go through life with masks on and our chests puffed out, giving this impression that we can handle anything. We can, if we have a refuge where a person loves us just as we are—no strings attached—just as God loves us!"

"My wife is awesome about making time for us. Taking care of four small children, home-schooling responsibilities, as well as her other involvements within the Christian community, she makes it a priority to arrange a date night once a week. Her commitment to making time for me shows me just how much she cares."

"A man needs something to go back to and for. My wife kept the fires burning—and burning brightly—for our sons and me, even when I was not there. I am always happy to go home! I know she is there with a big smile, a back rub, and a super meal she fixed with tender love. A man will die for that!"

"A man has to be able to return to something safe and stable. My wife has enabled me to focus on the important things in life at the time because of her unselfishness and love. In the past, it was surviving financial challenges, raising three sons, and running a business that was at first a success and then a failure. A man has to have someone around him who will let him try and fail, and try and succeed. I have done some really risky and ill-timed things in our life together. My wife has always remained my biggest cheerleader! And she does it with a smile! Wow!"

Remembering the Blessing . . .

It is not by chance that the very friendship these husbands so eloquently spoke of is by perfect design. As written in Genesis, the Lord Himself said it was not good for man to be alone. He needed a helper suitable for him—a friend and soul mate. Recall His miraculous and perfect plan as recorded in Genesis 2:21–23 NIV:

As best friends try to do, listen with a gentle heart and open mind, without casting judgment, to his struggles and failures. Remember, he is not necessarily looking for answers. He just needs a soft, safe place to land if only for a while until resuming his role as husband and father.

So the LORD God caused the man to fall into a deep sleep; and while he was sleeping, he took one of the man's ribs and closed up the place with flesh. Then the LORD God made a woman from the rib he had taken out of the man, and he brought her to the man. The man said,

"This is now bone of my bones
and flesh of my flesh;
she shall be called 'woman,'
for she was taken out of man."

God, in His infinite wisdom, *knew* it was not good for man to be alone. Not then. Not now. Not ever.

Are You Your Husband's Best Friend?

When brought to their attention, many wives admit to becoming so consumed with motherhood, they transferred the majority of their energy to the children. Sadly, it is not uncommon for a wife to also shift the friendship she once shared with her husband over to the children. Husbands feel the shift. Wives, typically, do not. Our busyness is blinding, making us unaware the shift has even occurred.

Have you unwittingly left your husband behind? Have you forgotten how to be a great wingman? How would your husband respond? Would he say that he feels the shift in your friendship?

He's busy too, you reason. He has his work, church involvements, and golf outings with the guys . . . and he hunts and fishes too!

Any or all of the above may be true, but would your husband say that you still empower him by the strength of your friendship, or is he seeking power via new venues? This may be one of the most important questions you ever ask yourself.

The longing of your husband's heart is for you to be his best friend. In my questionnaire, men were unexpectedly transparent, and their hearts surprisingly tender, on this topic. It was and is by God's perfect design that man not be alone, a reality our husbands readily embrace. Can you hear the cry of your husband's heart? Are you listening?

> *Edify your husband with words of encouragement and affirmation. Your love can and will empower him to be the man God is calling him to be. These words are effective when it's just the two of you but even more powerful when shared publicly. During the recent birthday celebration of my brother-in-law Steve Brode, my sister Amy toasted him as the man of honor he is. She spoke of his unwavering faith, commitment to family, and loyalty to friends. What a tender moment. What a wise woman. What a happy—truly happy—man.*

We need to nurture our marital friendship, keeping in mind, as one husband revealed, that men need a refuge—a person with whom they can be real. What a marvelous blessing the entire family receives when we edify our husband, motivating him to become a better man—the man God is calling him to be!

We know what to do. We did it all once upon a time, back when our love was beautiful and brand-new. Back in the days when being our husband's friend was what we did best. Yes, we know what to do. The only question remaining is, *will* we do it?

Reflection

Wise is the woman who nurtures the tender seedling of friendship in her marriage, for the overflow of blessings—her husband's love and devotion—are often only a heartbeat away.

There are three things that are too amazing for me,
*   four that I do not understand:*
the way of an eagle in the sky,
*   the way of a snake on a rock,*
the way of a ship on the high seas,
*   and the way of a man with a maiden.*

—Proverbs 30:18–19 NIV

As fair thou art, my bonnie lass,
So deep in love am I;
And I will love thee still, my dear,
Till a' the seas gang dry.

—Robert Burns

Chapter 6

Delight in Being the Beauty of His Life

IT IS A seldom-disputed fact that men fall in love with their eyes, while women fall in love with their ears. According to recent interviews I have conducted, when our husbands first met us, they were captivated by our beauty and femininity. In fact, many a husband claimed he felt powerless in our presence, smitten from the start—his heart ripe for the picking. Most shared that during courtship they found their intended to be stunningly beautiful, vibrant, cheerful, adventurous, witty, well read, gentle spirited, and yes, beautiful! Suffice it to say, our husbands were beguiled by the sheer marvel and miracle of we women.

> *Take a stroll down memory lane. Get a visual picture in your head of how you looked right before your now-husband picked you up for a date. Ask yourself: Am I still as conscientious about how I look when I go on a date with my husband?*

Is your beloved still beguiled by you? Or would *bewildered* be a more fitting description? How long has it been since you acknowledged the wonder of being a woman, and all that it entails? How long has it been since you embraced your own beauty? Can you recall the last time you had a facial, or a manicure, or a pedicure? My sisters and I used to give them to one another when we lived in the same city! If you can't remember the last time you marveled at the very wonder of your being a woman, your husband is noticing that you don't care about him enough to keep yourself attractive.

You're busy. Burdened. Exhausted from the endless list of commitments in your busy life. You may hold down a job, take care of your children, manage the household, sing in the church choir, car pool, serve as PTO president, volunteer with meals-on-wheels, and take your mother-in-law into town twice a week. And that's the short list.

Mirror, Mirror on the Wall

Take a moment to look in the mirror. Does the reflection staring back at you bear any resemblance to the woman your husband fell in love with some years ago? Is your hair styled in an attractive manner, or have you merely yanked it up in a clip without even brushing it? When was the last time you freshened your makeup, or have you not even bothered to apply any today? Are you wearing a clean, color-coordinated outfit, or a rumpled, mismatched warm-up suit two sizes too big?

> *Ask your husband what he appreciates or once appreciated about your physical appearance. Take it to heart and act on it!*

Our husbands still wish to delight in our femininity, in *all* of the wonder that makes us a woman. It's not some foolish fantasy. There is nothing more powerful or magical to a man than the femininity of the woman he married.

Note Solomon's testament to his bride's awe-inspiring beauty:

> *You are as beautiful as Tirzah, my darling,*
> *As lovely as Jerusalem,*
> *As awesome as an army with banners.*
>
> —Song of Solomon 6:4

Some months ago, I read John Eldredge's *Wild at Heart*. Surprisingly, it caught me off guard. Though it had earned terrific reviews, I'm not sure what I expected. Curled up in the well of my favorite window seat and ready for a good "read," the power of his message spoke to me. I was absolutely captivated by the book, especially chapter 10, "A Beauty to Rescue." Using poignant passages that leap off the pages and into the soul, Eldredge masterfully calls men to recover their masculine heart. In doing so, he reminds women that, by God's design, we encourage that process by remaining the beauty that first aroused and inspired our husbands to romance us — to be a hero for us.

My tears spilled shamelessly onto the pages of Eldredge's insights. On page 9 of *Wild at Heart*, he powerfully and poignantly describes a masculine heart when he writes:

> *God meant something when he meant man. . . . What has He set in the masculine heart? There are three desires I find written so deeply into my heart I know I can no longer disregard them without losing my soul. I am convinced these desires are universal, a clue into masculinity itself. They may be displaced, forgotten, or misdirected, but in the heart of every man is a desperate desire for a battle to fight, an adventure to live, and a beauty to rescue.*

Suddenly, I understood Bob's call to live out his masculine heart. It became *crystal clear* to me that when a man is truly in love, he will, at any cost, swim the ocean, climb the mountain, or slay the dragon for the woman he loves.

I reflected on my own ruggedly handsome husband. Then, without warning, thoughts of overwhelming tenderness tumbled into my mind: *Surely, the oceans Bob has swum, mountains he has scaled, and dragons he has slayed are too great in number to even count. And even after all these years he still considers me worth fighting for.*

With that, my thoughts continued tumbling in a backward spiral. I recalled the wisdom offered by our pastor many years ago during a premarital counseling session: "The chemistry and

> *This may require a shift in your time-management plan, but set aside thirty minutes a day, four days a week, for exercise. You will feel better and look better. Remember, beauty creates energy!*

passion you share is a great gift from God," he acknowledged with a knowing smile. He also cautioned that if chemistry and passion were neglected, that neglect would become a thorn that pricked at the core of our marriage.

Bob's heart was swept away by the beauty of my femininity. I was mesmerized by the mere thought of his masculinity—of him as my hero always prepared to defend my honor. Throwing caution to the wind, we chose chemistry over composure. Passion over playing it safe. And because of our affectionate natures, the essence of my womanhood was *very* much part of the picture, pastor counseled.

Burying Our Beauty

Then "real life" took over . . .

How easy it is to forget the magic of "once upon a time" in our lives when we wanted to look good for our husbands. Back in the days when we celebrated an inner *and* outer beauty that both inspired and nourished our beloved, *and* gave glory to the God who created us!

> *Look through a magazine to see what new beauty products are available. Every so often, treat yourself to one that makes you embrace your femininity.*

Perhaps we forget because of shuttling children from baseball to ballet. Or because we work back-to-back shifts at the hospital and have nurse's reports to complete before we can even shuttle the children. Or we've stood all day in a classroom teaching wiggly third graders—leaving little energy for pampering ourselves. But somehow or somewhere along the way, delighting in our husband's appreciation of our feminity dropped *way* down on our priority list.

> *Treat yourself to a day at the spa, or have a girlfriend with great style do your hair, makeup, and nails. This will be fun for you, and it will be fun to see the look on your husband's face when he sees you!*

Think back to the days when your husband courted you. Remember when you wooed your love? Chances are slim to none you greeted him for a date with grubby hair, grimy teeth, and a soiled sweat suit. You wanted to entice him with your physical appearance. It mattered then. You intuitively understood that the magic of your beauty inspired and energized your man.

An attractive forty-something career journalist recently confided that her husband had for years been hinting that he missed the way she used to look. "It hurt to discover my appearance meant so much to him until I took a long look at myself and decided to lose twenty pounds. Now, a year later, I realize that his approach was the only way he knew to express his need for me to remain the object of his desire. He was asking me to take the effort to look good for him— to show him that *he* was still the object of my desire."

> *Remember to praise God for your birthright. You are a fearfully-and-wonderfully-made, beautiful daughter of the King!*

Through Their Eyes . . .

One husband of twenty years shared: "A woman's physical appearance, good or bad, is always noticed. It may seem shallow, but that is the way we, as men, process things. It's part of who we are and how we were created. Take the passages in Solomon's Song of Songs for example. The point is made *over* and *over* and *over* again that a man appreciates physical beauty. And though I don't always verbalize my appreciation for my wife's beauty, it doesn't mean I'm not thinking about it. It's always on my mind!"

Thoughts from another husband: "I married the most beautiful girl in the world. More than fifty years later, I am still married to the most beautiful girl in the world. I appreciate how she takes care of herself. In turn, it causes me to keep myself in shape for her. Mind you, her beauty is different at seventy-five than it was at twenty-one. She carries herself with such grace, I nearly cry each time I see her."

And still another: "Alright. You asked for it, so here goes. This is what I wish I could say to my wife but can't. It feels somewhat like a betrayal on my part, but if I don't say this now, I'm afraid I never will. . . . If all I wanted was someone to cook, clean, chauffeur the children, and work on every committee in town, I would have hired someone to do just that. In fact, I would have hired more than one person and not cared how they look. A worn-out worker is not what I want. But my wife can't seem to say 'no' to anyone from the church, community, or the children's school. She doesn't have time to be the attractive woman I married. I miss the spark her beauty used to bring to our marriage. And I am willing to do whatever it takes for her to find time to take better care of herself."

The truth hurts, doesn't it? Like it or not, we all need to take some ownership of that disclosure. At one time or another we have been that wife. Sisters in Christ, we *must* listen to the longings of our husband's heart, especially if the above passage strikes a nerve. Even more so if we think it couldn't possibly apply to us.

Husbands are pleading with us on this issue. It isn't that they don't appreciate our countless obligations, but they fear we will allow the strains of our busy lifestyle to extinguish the beauty of the women we are. They want us to remember that our physical appearance is important to them. What's more, they want it to be important to us too! Additionally, we should, on a regular basis, remember what it is that appeals to our husband about our appearance—and act on it! Can't remember what appeals to him most? Why not ask him.

The Look of Love

Last Valentine's Day, Candy and Dave flew out to Big Bear, California, for a work-related seminar and a much-needed romantic ski getaway. Having barely guided their eighteen-year-old son through an especially trying teenage phase, they were exhausted.

> *Discard your shabby and sloppy clothing—the comfy, cozy, dreary outfits you are saving for posterity's sake. The ones you slip into in the evenings and sometimes wear to bed. While you're at it, cut up your oversized flannel nightgowns with the frayed edges and toss them in the rag bag. Invest in two new nightgowns—one that makes you blush and one that makes you smile—and wear them!*

By her own admission, the emotional wear and tear was most obvious on Candy. Taking the time to pamper herself, however, the way she always had when she was dating Dave, inspired him to romance her in a way that, to this day, brings a smile to her face.

Walking down the steps at the ski resort, Candy planned to grab a hot chocolate when she caught Dave staring at her from his vantage point at the top of the stairway. He had a most unusual and tender look on his face. Embarrassed, Candy felt the color rising in her cheeks.

"What?" she squeaked as she searched his face for an explanation. His eyes said everything her heart needed to hear. You see, by scooping her hair into a ponytail and wearing a favorite sweater she knew he liked on her, Candy let him know that he was still important to her. Dave knew she had dressed with him in mind, and he loved it. His eyes said what his words did not. That reaction is important for us to remember when our husband is not able to articulate what he sees and feels. Often, a look says what words cannot.

Dave's reaction to Candy was a perfect reminder that, next to God, we wives should most want to please our husbands. His reaction was also a reminder that men are extremely visual creatures deeply appreciative of "feminine beauty."

Beauty Is Our Heavenly Birthright

In Psalm 139:14, we are reminded that we are fearfully and wonderfully made. What a blessing to exemplify the very essence of God, in whose image we were created! This should leave no doubt that our beauty is by perfect design. For, not only is a gentle, joyous spirit the trademark of a godly woman, so too is the unique and extraordinary beauty God bestowed upon us. Our external beauty is a mere expression of our internal beauty. Indeed, the very core of our internal beauty as tender, nurturing, uniquely feminine beings is our heavenly birthright.

If, *today*, your husband were to spy you strolling down the street for the very first time, would he want to meet you all over again?

Will you delight once again in being the beauty in your husband's life? Keep in mind that your husband is created for and charged with the responsibility to love, protect, and lead you. It's part of his masculine leadership mandated in Scripture. Yet, your femininity—in all his masculine ways—causes him to feel weak-kneed. He certainly doesn't understand why this happens. He's a creature of logic. He just knows the sight of you can still make his knees buckle! Will you love him enough to inspire his call to live out his masculine heart just as God designed him to do?

Reflection

If a gentle, joyous spirit is the trademark of a godly woman, so too is our embracing the unique and extraordinary beauty God bestowed upon us at birth. Truly delight in being the beauty in your husband's life!

You will go out in joy
and be led forth in peace;
the mountains and hills
will burst into song before you,
and all the trees of the field
will clap their hands.

—Isaiah 55:12 NIV

Home interprets heaven; home is heaven for beginners.

—Charles Henry Parkhurst

Chapter 7

Rest, Relaxation, and a Little Recreation

THINK BACK ONCE again to those days of "wine and roses" with your new husband, back to the days when the breath of dawn and the promise of a day bathed in brilliant sunshine was all it took to draw you outdoors. Remember romantic picnics in the park—the ones with fried chicken, potato salad, lemonade, and apple pie?

After tossing the Frisbee around for hours, you'd stretch out on a fabric-softener fresh blanket, exchanging easy conversation. The sound of laughter rang across the sweet summer breeze. You barely noticed as the afternoon sun slipped behind the trees. Snuggled side by side, you and your beloved beheld, and vowed you'd never forget, the beauty of the breathtaking airbrushed dusk, the sky streaked with peach, plum, and magenta.

Shaking crumbs from the blanket as you prepared to leave, the twinkling of starlight illuminated your way to the car. Remember the feeling of that perfect, peaceful bliss? Rested and refreshed, you were ready to face the world with renewed vigor. That romantic encounter, and later its recollection, refreshed you through and through. These outings were sanctuaries that soothed your souls.

The High Cost of Busyness

When did we become too busy to rest? Too burdened to relax? And when did taking "time out" to have fun fall out of fashion? Did it vanish somewhere between babies one and two? Did it disappear in a paper pile of mortgage payments and credit card bills?

If we can't even remember the last time we took time out to relax, it's a sure bet we need to be reminded of another long-known fact:

Exhaustion—lack of rest and relaxation—physically, emotionally, and spiritually weakens us. And given that, it is time to get to the heart of the matter: what effect is our exhaustion and lack of rest having on our marriages?

If we examine our lives closely, we may see that our incessant busyness is wearing away the well-being of our marriages, one activity at a time. Exhaustion clearly controls many marriages.

Look and Listen for What He Doesn't Say

Wives, our complaint of "no time" for rest, relaxation, and recreation suggests we have no power. Nothing could be further from the truth. Our husbands are weary from the hours of working and the worries that go hand in hand in their roles as providers. They need to be steered to a shelter, a refuge from the relentless storms of life. And while they may not articulate that need, we need only look a little closer to see the truth.

> *With your husband, take turns on alternate months to plan a secret adventure for the two of you. It can be as playful as spending the morning visiting his favorite aquarium or as simple as sharing an ice-cream soda while sitting on a park bench.*

Look at your beloved tonight. Has the battle of incessant busyness taken its toll on him? *He doesn't look angry or resentful,* you reason silently. *And I'm just as tired as he is.* Look again, this time with a tender spirit and open heart. Could his "serene" expression, shoulders slightly slumped, suggest instead his simple but poignant resignation that permanent fatigue has taken up residence in your marriage?

It would appear so . . .

"I'm so beaten down by the end of the day. I don't have the energy to even *entertain* the thought of relaxation or recreation. Rest—just enough to get me to the next day—is my primary need," shared one obviously weary husband and father of three.

"I feel guilty at this stage of the game," admitted another husband. "There are some nights when I collapse on the couch as soon as I walk through the door. Particularly after an especially grueling business trip. I know my wife is tired too, but honestly, my fatigue overpowers my desire to lighten her load."

"I'm going to sound like the ogre of the group, but I *can't* rest when I come home from work. Our house is covered with, not only our children, but the neighborhood children—literally. And while, for the most part, I welcome them into our place, I need time before dinner to unwind. A quiet corner is nonexistent at that time of day. The kids are still very much in charge. And as far as relaxation and recreation are concerned, I'm afraid they are no longer a priority. I sure hope that changes. I miss that element of our lives and guess I had always depended on my wife's leading in that area."

How does your daily planner look? Is it filled with overlapping appointments and social engagements? With a discerning heart, start pruning your schedule. Much of it is a misguided overdose of our I-must-be-busy-until-I-drop mentality. Chaos and confusion are but two of our most draining daily contenders. Why not make a conscious decision to bless your husband with a simpler, more balanced life?

"The greatest gift my wonderful wife could give me regarding rest is to welcome me home to a calm house. I am in desperate need of a 'sanctuary' at the end of the day. If she could provide me with a peaceful time to recharge my batteries, I feel I could, in turn, give her the break she needs. As far as relaxation and recreation go, I miss our off-season picnics on the beach, bike rides, and making fudge together."

"Rest, relaxation, and recreation with my wife? You name it. I'm all hers!"

Is the Grass Really Greener on the Other Side?

Ironically, the current trend in home decorating is creating a home that is a haven—a sanctuary for the everyday celebrations of life. Would your husband say your home is a haven?

As a bona fide hit-the-floor-running sanguine personality, understanding my husband's need for rest required that I step out of myself. After all, I stayed at home with three active children during the day, and he had fun jetting around the country. When Bob arrived home, I was ready to continue where the kids and I left off in whatever activity presented itself. *Why does he look so tired when all he does is accumulate frequent-flyer miles?* I wondered.

Then one day I flew to Virginia to attend a seminar sponsored by The National Society of Newspaper Columnists. Like a sponge, I absorbed every drop of knowledge presented. One unexpected bit of knowledge I returned home with, however, proved to be the pivotal point in my marriage. Jetting around the country for business purposes was grueling. Five days at my seminar educated me in areas I hadn't intended. I felt exhausted from information overload. The two-hour return flight offered me the much-needed opportunity to reflect on my exhaustion and my profound longing for the sweet sanctuary of our home.

Sadly, it was my own experience that took me to that place of reflection. Yet, isn't it our time of reflection that gives our experiences the power to change us? *So this is the "real-life" version of what happens when Bob is away,* I thought. *No wonder the poor guy craves a quiet corner when he comes home.* And as my plane touched down on the runway at Orlando International Airport, home was the only thing on my mind.

> *Interested in another way to help your husband relax and fill his desire to be informed, educated, and inspired? What does your husband enjoy reading? Periodicals, novels, historical accounts? If he is not much of a reader, would he perhaps enjoy a book on tape? If you have not already done so, familiarize yourself with your public library. Check out books or books on tape for your sweetie. Only a click away, you can order his favorite trilogy on Amazon's Web site. Or the hunting and fishing periodical he grabs from his brother's house every month. Encourage the environment needed for a good read!*

Home, and how, from that day forward, our home would be a sweet sanctuary for my husband and a veritable resting place for his weary heart.

Make Your Home into a Haven

I started by sending the neighbor children to their respective homes when Bob came home at night. Granting him a mere fifteen minutes to unwind gave him the second wind he needed to make it through the activities of the night—joyfully. In turn, he was willing and anxious to bless me by assisting me with whatever tasks I had yet to tackle. Each week, I initiated another way to "ease" him into the evening hours: simple things that relaxed and blessed him such as a back rub, freshly brewed sweet tea, an additional night at the gym, or sometimes, the luxury of watching a blood-and-guts war movie at night all by himself. Some time ago, Bob shared with me that those extra installments of consideration fortified him enough to "stay the course" during the most demanding season of our lives.

Creating a haven is an ongoing process. Last month we made an unplanned move. Engineers had, only days earlier, determined our home was not structurally safe due to the damage incurred from our three hurricanes. In just three weeks, we began the mortgage process and search for a new home, found and signed a contract on another home, found a moving company,

> *Designate quiet time—downtime—which allows your husband, and you, to catch your breath after work and a busy day. Sometimes this is enough to give your husband a second wind until bedtime. Send the neighborhood children home, thus giving the clear message that family time has begun.*

packed, and moved in. We felt like we had been dragged around by the tail end of another hurricane! When the boys came home from university that first weekend they brought their usual entourage of friends. One room at a time was taken over by the loveable Florida State gang, and, before long, Bob was all but displaced. He couldn't find a quiet spot in the house. He was exhausted and in desperate need of peace and quiet. Though he rarely becomes agitated, he reacted like a grizzly bear. Yes, he even roared!

After having had a marvelous time, and completely unaware the grizzly had been agitated, the guys decided to return home the following weekend. But this time I made certain the college crowd understood there were courtesies and considerations they had to abide by if they wanted to enjoy the blessings of our lakefront home. Though I want our home to be enjoyed by all, it is still our haven. And after being displaced, I will need to be especially sensitive to making our new home the resting place Bob so desperately needs.

What changes can you make to your home so that it is a haven—a resting place for your husband's weary heart? Ask him. Based on the responses of the men interviewed, he will be only too happy to tell you!

If your budget is on the lean side at this time, how about this terrific idea for a romantic night at home? One of you works on putting the children to bed, while the other prepares the "grown-up" dinner. Once the little ones are asleep, you and your husband can enjoy a romantic, candle-lit dinner for two without the additional cost of a babysitter or restaurant check. Note: This might be one of those days where the wee ones' naptime is kept to a minimum. You don't want to start your romantic evening so late you're both falling asleep during your main course!

Remember to listen with your heart, not just your head. Keep in mind it is more than possible that by blessing him with quiet time to unwind and recharge, he may be motivated to reciprocate the blessing. Kindness truly does beget kindness!

Take Time for Fun

Have you heard that reflection is the midwife of wisdom? Here's the great part: we don't even need to birth new ideas! We need only recall those moments of wonder we created when we first wooed our husbands. That's the beauty of taking time out for reflection. It reminds us of our need to get back to basics, to firm up the very foundation we began building upon, the one that worked quite well once upon a time.

Rest, relaxation, and recreation, we have established, are essential to our well-being. But knowing is only half the battle. And we have yet to touch on recreation—having fun with our husband the way we once did. Fill in the blank to finish the following sentence: The last time my husband and I planned, and followed through on, a fun day for just the two of us, we _____.

Did you struggle to fill in the blank? If so, it's okay. It's only natural to get caught up in the everyday events of life. And the thought of adding recreation to our already overcrowded schedules is no laughing matter, which is precisely the point. Would your husband say you are still fun? That you are still the one who makes him laugh?

Marriage Is a Marathon, Not a Sprint

It took me longer than most to realize it was necessary for Bob and me to have our own playtime. The grueling pace was taking its toll on us. Marriage, I discovered, is much like a marathon. To go the distance, one must set a realistic pace. Looking back, it is frightening to realize how I had turned from a fun-loving wife and mother to a tense, tight-lipped taskmaster. Erroneously, I had assumed that plugging "fun" into Mommy and Daddy's world would only take away from the quality of our family life. Nothing—absolutely nothing— could have been further from the truth!

I reintroduced playtime into our marriage with simple things like surprise picnics, bicycle rides, and walks on the beach to collect shells. As our budget grew and our responsibilities shrank (the boys were off to college), we began skiing out West and fishing in Canada. (As I type this paragraph, I am sitting fireside after a day of fishing in a forty-something degree ice-cold rain. And you know what? In spite of the cold and rain, the fish were biting, and we had a blast making memories that strengthen our marriage.)

Has it been awhile since you last heard the sound of your own laughter? What about the sound of your husband's laughter? Remember back when you first dated, how the sound of each other's laughter made your love grow even stronger?

Go back to the beginning. What forms of recreation did you and your husband enjoy before bills and babies took hold?

Your husband wants you to know he misses your tenderness. He misses the ways you used to nurture him. He needs a refuge, a safe place to rest his weary head and, at times, heavy heart. Emotional well-being and warmth of home and hearth is vital to him. He has lovingly placed his longings before you. How will you answer his pleas? Will you take time today to restore the three Rs—rest, relaxation, and recreation—to their rightful place in your marriage?

Reflection

Implement the three Rs into your lifestyle—those "sanctuaries" that soothe the soul. In doing so, you invite your husband to embrace the everyday epiphanies that make home a haven.

Anger is cruel, and wrath is like a flood, but who can survive the destructiveness of jealousy?

— Proverbs 27:4 NLT

Jealousy is . . . a tiger that tears not only at its prey but also its own raging heart.

— Michael Beer

Chapter 8

Master the Monster Called Jealousy

J EALOUSY. WHAT AN ugly word. What an ugly emotion. The very word implies weakness, worry, and wreckage. As Solomon warns us in Proverbs 27:4, "Anger is cruel, and wrath is like a flood, but who can survive the destructiveness of jealousy?" (NLT)

Thirty-three-year-old insurance agent Paige, a survivor of jealousy's wrath, knows that many women fall prey to this monster and hopes her well-earned wisdom will help them slay their own monster once and for all.

A Monster Is Born

Her jealousy began with the breakdown of her first marriage after she discovered her husband had been unfaithful to her. The jealousy she felt toward this woman, who, in Paige's eyes, stole her husband, was mind-boggling. Even though she knew her husband had made the same choices as the "other woman," it was easier to blame the woman for the affair. As time went on, Paige's jealousy turned into insecurity, insecurity into self-doubt. *What was it about me?* she wondered. *Was I not pretty enough? Not thin enough? Was it my hair? My personality? Our love life? What then?*

Not having answers for the questions that plagued her, Paige tumbled in a downward spiral. Before long she began what would be a pain-filled journey.

Do you know how, when you're disappointed and disillusioned, you wonder what your place in the world is? That's what Paige did. She anguished over why she wasn't good enough to be loved by a man who vowed to love and cherish her "until death do us part." Because her heartache, loneliness, and betrayal became a stronghold, Paige began trudging through her pain wearing "brokenhearted shoes." Imagine, trudging through knee-high sludge in the aftermath of a hurricane, each step exhausting, and at times, painful. So too was Paige's journey, trodding through life wearing brokenhearted shoes. And then she did what she thought was best: she buried the pain deep in her heart, convincing herself her brokenheartedness had come to an end.

Jealousy Knows No Bounds

Fast-forward to a blessed second chance at love and marriage. Paige is now the wife of a wonderful, godly man who is the prophet, priest, and king of their home. He loves, honors, and cherishes her. What more could she want?

> *Jealousy can be fatal to a relationship. On the other hand, healthy boundaries promote healthy relationships. Discuss and clearly understand what situations you and your husband feel comfortable with. Honor those boundaries, erring always on the side of caution.*

"In the beginning, I wanted for him to not have a first wife, child, and past with someone other than me. Never mind that I had the same! At first, my husband and I argued because of my insecurities, which, of course, once again led to low self-esteem. Jealousy even appeared in my relationship with my stepdaughter because of her closeness to her mother! Jealousy knows no bounds. It doesn't discriminate between lovers, parents, children, siblings, and friends."

After three years, many prayers, and much validation from those who love her, Paige has a more accurate view of who she is. But, as she also learned, it is only through Christ's eyes that she is able to see herself for whom He created her to be.

Jealousy is not rational thinking. It is an emotion of the heart—an evil-eyed monster tapping on our soul and whispering doubts into our ear. Jealousy, according to Paige, is the key Satan uses to gain access to our hearts and, when he does, we become his playground. His toys are self-doubt, low self-esteem, lack of validation, and other such lies. These toys keep Satan quite busy. Sometimes he packs a picnic and stays all day in our playground of self-doubt and low self-esteem.

Forgetting to lock the gate to our heart and hand Christ the key is a huge mistake! Satan, knowing there is no curfew, simply opens the gate and enters at will. As happened with Paige, Satan laughed at the destruction, while Paige wept over the consequences. It's only when we look at ourselves through Christ's eyes that we recognize who we are and Whose we are. And, once again, God gains access to our heart, locking out the monster of jealousy.

"It took *really* knowing and believing who I am and *Whose* I am to finally slay the monster," Paige concluded, struggling to keep her voice from breaking. "But because I now know, I no longer walk through life wearing brokenhearted shoes."

The State of Our Hearts

Did you feel the passion in Paige's voice and sense the depth of her struggle? Read the words as though they were your own. Even if jealousy is not something you wrestle with, our weaknesses are enough to sabotage us. So let's arm ourselves with the weapons and wisdom necessary to slay this monster should it ever begin pursuing us.

Jealousy is an emotion of the heart. Though we are frequently encouraged to "follow our heart," our emotions, especially if damaged, are not always reliable or accurate. Because the heart is also our "control center," our emotions play a major part in our reactions and decision-making process. Our emotions vacillate and our feelings fluctuate. It's important to remember, as written in Jeremiah 17:9, "The heart is deceitful above all things" (NIV).

Lest we question the weight of Jeremiah's words, remember that even in a more or less benign, but sensitive, situation requiring honest communication between husband and wife, our emotions have a tendency to run high!

> *If you wrestle with jealousy, pray that you see the truth of your situation and seek wisdom from another woman who can walk you through the healing process. While honesty is essential, hold "your cards" close to your heart as far as with whom you share your struggle. You need not reveal everything to everyone. Some things are meant to be kept "sacred." Retain your dignity and your husband's. Remember, flaws included, you are children of the King!*

Liv was enjoying dinner with her husband of twenty-nine years when a "strikingly beautiful" woman was seated nearby. Her husband could not stop looking at her.

"I was looking at her too," added Liv, "but *his* looking and *my* looking took on two different meanings. By the time we made it home I was livid. Fit to be tied. I told him I felt that he had cheated on me with his eyes. While a glance or two is acceptable, he had passed the point of what was acceptable. Though he apologized over and over again, it took me awhile before I got over it. Trust is as valuable as diamonds, and we, as husbands and wives, need to continually respond to each other's strengths and weaknesses. I should mention that he is a fantastic husband and since that night he has asked that if I feel uncomfortable in any situation I need to let him know and he will respond at once. In hindsight, I allowed my emotions to carry me too far. It was a bad night. A very bad night . . ."

> *We are responsible for maintaining the health of our own self-worth. Remember, what we "feed" ourselves spiritually and emotionally greatly affects our perception of "who" we are. Do your reading materials and media entertainment choices reflect your living in the world or of the world?*

Remember, an injured heart is Satan's playground. When he is able to gain access, he toys with our emotions, whispering lies in our ears. He doesn't distinguish between strong and weak marriages, secure or wounded women.

Bound by Satan's Lies

Are you ever taunted by the subtle "whisper" of these lies?

"Oh wow . . . she's beautiful! He can't resist gawking at her. You don't look that good."

"Girl, your father—your own father—strayed. Men stray. This is reality!"

"Remember, your first love cheated on you, and he said he loved you. Do you actually think your husband will always remain faithful?"

"You're weak. Do you really think you can overcome your insecurity? After all, you've already tried a hundred times. Accept it. It's just who you are."

Sadly, when we are trudging along, walking in brokenhearted shoes, we *do* accept these lies as truths. In the pain of our journey, we forget just who we are. We forget that if our heavenly Father could part the Red Sea, surely He cares enough to free us from the bondage of lies. It is not God's plan for us that we remain enslaved to sin. But first we need truth. As Jesus said in John 8:32, "You will know the truth, and the truth will make you free."

> *Idle gossip is not a reliable source of information. Frequently, information passes through several venues before reaching our ears. What's more important, it's rarely accurate. Trust your husband unless there is a solid reason not to!*

What Is Truth?

Here's where that truth is vitally important, and each of us must do the excavation required within ourselves: Did you enter your marriage with unresolved emotional wounds from the past? Often, we're unaware of the depth of those wounds. We fool ourselves into thinking they're buried in the layers of our past. In reality, those wounds lay just beneath the surface, resurfacing again and again.

Imagine that you purchase a beautiful pair of leather Italian loafers. With proper care they should last a lifetime. A special oil to protect the leather is included with your purchase. Regular treatment is recommended to ensure the life of the shoes. But by and by, you get busy, a little lazy, and yes, a little careless too. You're not as careful with the shoes as you once were. Not even applying the oil protector anymore, you slosh through rain, take shortcuts through snow, and, instead of drying them properly,

> *Stay grounded in not only who you are but also in "Whose you are." Don't permit yourself to be caught and held captive by Satan's lies. Spiritual truths rule!*

you sling them haphazardly in the garage each time. Then one day you slip your feet into your shoes and are shocked to see the soles are doing this little "slap, slap, slap," as you walk. Looking down, you're shocked to see they need new soles. You can't believe how dingy and dirty they've become. They're also all you have. Ashamed and embarrassed, you understand the reality: at least for the foreseeable future, you must walk in broken shoes.

Is it any different with your heart? If you're feeling the "slap, slap, slap" of your broken "shoes," or if the "soles" are showing signs of wear and tear, perhaps that monster called jealousy has chased you long enough.

Do the whispers of "you're not pretty, thin, smart, talented, (you fill in the blank)" tear your heart down? If so, with what do you counter them? If you don't counter these lies with truth, the downward spiral Paige spoke of earlier begins. And without warning, you too are trudging through life wearing brokenhearted shoes.

But if you know who you are and Whose you are, Satan loses his stronghold over your heart. John 10:10 says, "The thief comes only to steal and kill and destroy; I came that they may have life, and have it abundantly."

Realize jealousy is a by-product of the wayward thinking we've latched onto somewhere along life's journey. Sadly, such thoughts usually take on life-forms of their own. Amazingly though, releasing the death grip on such thoughts often takes the life right out of them!

The truth is that you are a princess, a daughter of the King. He thinks you are beautiful, lovely, warm, witty, capable, and worthy. He is absolutely delighted in and by you! Reflect on Isaiah 62:3: "You will also be a crown of beauty in the hand of the LORD, and a royal diadem in the hand of your God." Don't you see? He longs for you to wear dancing shoes—not brokenhearted shoes! His desire is that your heart dance with delight simply because you know Whose you are.

Men's Thoughts on Jealousy

Interestingly, jealousy is one topic where you might say husbands lack understanding and discernment. At times, as I "read between the lines" of their responses, they might as well have said, "I don't understand jealousy, and I don't ever want to be in the position where I have to!" Jealousy seems to stump them—frighten them—which is why it is so important that Paige was willing to open her heart for all to see.

Just to give you an idea though, most husbands who did respond to the survey agreed with the following statements:

"Jealousy is one of Satan's favorite tools. I believe the responsibility lies with the husband to exhibit genuine evidence there is nothing to worry about on the part of the wife. In my humble opinion, people do not normally feel jealous without a reason."

"Wives, tell your husbands what you are comfortable and not comfortable with, this way your husband will avoid the situations you and he are not comfortable with. For example, I do not dance with another woman (even a friend) if my wife is not present. Communication is very important to me, but on this topic of jealousy, a wife needs to look at her husband's track record—not just at the moment or particular incident. If they do this, I feel, in most cases, they'll see the love their husband has for them."

> *I recommend Jerry B. Jenkins's* Loving Your Marriage Enough to Protect It *(Chicago: Moody, 1993). One chapter deals with the dangers of flirting and the emotions stirred up that should be only for a spouse.*

"Oh boy . . . I don't know what I'd do if jealousy were ever a problem with my wife. I really don't."

Putting Wisdom to Work

Let's put our wisdom to work! If a situation arises with our husband where we feel uncomfortable or threatened, we have two choices: We can freak out. Turn into hand-wringing, clingy creatures. Scream, yell, and stomp our feet. (How much dignity is there in *that*?) We can take our "homegrown" fear and feed it, which causes it to take on a life-form of its own, and we wonder how that little emotion grew too big to handle.

Or we can walk in wisdom. We can state our concerns clearly and calmly, communicating exactly what it is that hurts or offends us. To do so requires that we be spiritually grounded in the truth. Keep in mind that our doing so doesn't necessarily guarantee the outcome. Much depends on the spiritual maturity of our husband and the seriousness of the situation. But by being spiritually grounded, we are equipped to handle a potentially relationship-threatening situation with the grace and dignity of who we were created to be—daughters of the King.

Some situations may require professional counsel. If that is the case, please do not hesitate to seek it. But a good place to start is to remember how very much God loves you.

There isn't a man alive who wants a jealous, insecure woman by his side. It's demeaning to both husband and wife. Likewise, there isn't a woman alive who wants to feel jealous or insecure. And while each situation is unique and would take more time and paper than this book allows, we know that both insecurity and jealousy usually result from errant thoughts stemming from a wayward world, past wounds, and lies.

A Father's Gift

If today, you are trudging through life wearing brokenhearted shoes—or even if they're just a bit worn—your Father has a gift for you. God loves you so. He created marriage for you and wants to bless you and your husband beyond your wildest dreams. He wants to replace your brokenhearted shoes with dancing shoes because He united you, His beloved daughter, with His favored son in marriage. To Him, you are beautiful, lovely, warm, witty, and worthy. He knows you will wear them well.

Reflection

A fear-based emotion, jealousy is an external symptom of an internal injury. It holds the heart and soul captive. Heal the heart and free the soul.

See to it that no one comes short of the grace of God; that no root of bitterness springing up causes trouble, and by it many be defiled.

—Hebrews 12:15

Forgiveness is a key element in healthy long-term marriages. Forgiveness is the oil that lubricates a love relationship, and it's an oil we need daily. Forgiveness is not a one-time event; it's an attitude of wanting to partner with your spouse in spite of his or her imperfections and irritations.

—David and Claudia Arp

Chapter 9

Practice the Power of Forgiveness

I COULDN'T HAVE been more than sixteen when a friend I deeply admired shared the following with me: "It takes a lot to make me mad, but once you've made me mad, it might take a lifetime for me to forgive and forget. And I may never *really* forget."

If she feels this way, it must not be possible to forgive and forget, I reasoned. Unknowingly, I instilled that perspective deep into the heart of my own internal value system. It took many years before I would hear a story of such love and forgiveness that it would overwrite the core of my own value system. The following is Caroline's story, the story that changed my life.

Broken Dreams

It was the night before Christmas. A soft blanket of snow had just begun to cover the earth when Caroline accidentally uncovered a secret that would forever change her life: Kurt, her beloved husband of twenty-six years, had been unfaithful.

Devastated by his deception, Caroline curled up in a fetal position in a corner of their bedroom floor. In the living room, Kurt led their four children through the motions of their Christmas Eve traditions, the children aware that something was terribly wrong.

Plotting her righteous revenge, Caroline was already planning a divorce. Then, hoping she would awaken from what was only a bad dream, muffled sounds of her children's cries jolted her back to reality. It was then she sensed a still, small voice "whispering" to her heart. Her body stiffened. In a moment of defiance, Caroline hoped it wasn't God. She was too angry for divine intervention. After all, she wasn't the one who had strayed from God or marriage. And just where was He while Kurt strayed? No, Caroline did not want that "nudging" to be from the Father she felt had forgotten her. Let Him work on Kurt. He was the one in need of the divine intervention.

As much as Caroline tried to ignore that still, small voice, she could not. Was God trying to get her attention? It had to be Him, because the thoughts in her heart were all about love and forgiveness. She, by her own admission, was incapable of initiating any thoughts of forgiveness. Revenge, rather than reconciliation, consumed her heart tonight.

Caroline, the small voice seemed to whisper, *you hold the pen of life in your hand. It is you and only you who must write the words to this script, you who will create an ending to this story.*

Wrapping a worn afghan around her shoulders, wave after wave of grief washed over her. She fought to remember exactly when she and the man she loved became two strangers living under one roof. Trembling harder with each incoming set of sobs, Caroline wondered: Is this what is to become of us now? Nothing more than a mediocre marriage shattered by the unthinkable?

> *Wipe the ledger of your husband's transgressions clean. If necessary, write those bigger-than-life moments when he has hurt you down on a piece of paper, and then burn it! Do whatever you must do to put the past behind you.*

Hadn't she sensed a hollow silence between them? That they had grown indifferent to each other? Or even that, for quite some time, her husband had tried in vain to re-create the magic that once existed between them?

"I miss *us*, Caroline," Kurt had confided in her some time ago. "I miss spending time together. We used to walk and talk for hours on the trail, and it was so easy to laugh with you. That's my first memory of you—seeing you with your head thrown back and laughing—from across the room in the campus coffee shop. Now, it seems the kids and the girls at your office have taken my place."

Trying to force the memory of Kurt's words from her mind was useless. Instead, truth tore at her heart. She *had* been too busy as a pharmaceutical rep and as mother tending to the needs of four children to pay much attention to her husband. As though he were little more than an afterthought, she gave to Kurt only what she had left at the end of each day. And *that*, she realized, had been very little.

When she'd accepted the pharmaceutical position five years earlier, she'd had the best of intentions. She had been confident that, with her degree and exceptional organizational skills, she could manage a family and a demanding career. *I've worked hard for this,* she had reasoned. And the additional income had provided the family with those perks they had grown to expect. After all, it was all about family, wasn't it?

Love Can Find a Way

Still curled up on that hard, cold floor, Caroline faced a hard, cold reality: she'd ignored nearly all of Kurt's basic needs—for years. And she'd sent him straight

> *Commit to prayer those areas of weakness and unforgiving attitudes in your heart that allow bitterness to seep in.*

into the arms of a woman who was more than willing to provide the emotional and physical intimacy she'd withheld. She was as much to blame as her husband.

In the wee hours of the morning, she gathered the courage to summon Kurt. Kneeling on the floor beside her with his head bowed in her lap, he tearfully begged for his wife's forgiveness.

In less than an hour, Christmas morning would dawn. Now nestled in an overstuffed easy chair by the Christmas tree, sipping a cup of herbal tea, Caroline thought of her children. If she chose to, she could give her family the gift they wanted most, the gift of a future together.

So . . . it all comes down to this, she reasoned. *I hold the pen, and I'm the one who writes the script. Why is it always the one who is hurt the most who has to give the most?* Caroline grappled.

In what would be the most powerful moment of their marriage, Caroline chose to forgive her husband. Realizing the journey ahead would be filled with many challenges, she opted to embrace the future rather than cling to the past. While the pain from Kurt's unfaithfulness was almost more than she could bear, she knew that, without forgiveness, bitterness is all they would have to show for a lifetime of love.

So, on the tattered pages of her husband's heart, she inscribed the words, *I forgive you.* She trusted that God, the Father of forgiveness, would guide her to write the rest.

Will you write, *I forgive you*, on the pages of your husband's heart?

Beware of "Little Foxes"

Whether or not we've suffered the agony of adultery, one fact still remains: every marriage is full of those more subtle transgressions that gnaw at our relationship. We are reminded in Song of Solomon that those "little foxes" are the kinds of problems that can diminish or destroy a relationship.

> *Catch the foxes for us,*
> *The little foxes that are ruining the vineyards,*
> *While our vineyards are in blossom.*
>
> —Song of Solomon 2:15

Those "little foxes" include the times when your husband is rude to you in front of your family. Or when, on the rare opportunity you have to talk to him at night, he's more interested in the tying run on second than he is in your crisis with a coworker. Perhaps your husband is a workaholic and the intimacy in your marriage has turned into isolation. Or he doesn't back you up in your decision on an issue with one of the children. Or, here's one, he enjoys a day of leisure on the golf course—on *your* birthday! Your initial hurt has turned to anger, and you have silently declared the topic off-limits.

> *Discuss with your husband those instances or areas where you still struggle and find forgiveness difficult. Remember, he is not a mind reader!*

For years I struggled with the concept of *true* forgiveness, even in the more commonplace issues just mentioned. Whenever I wrote *I forgive you* on the pages of Bob's heart, I must have used a washable marker, for I had the tendency of resurrecting his past failures and flinging them back at him in the heat of an argument—until Caroline shared her story, that is.

For me, Caroline's story illustrates, in a most poignant way, the power of pardon and that forgiveness is a choice. And I, like many other women who have heard her story, knew there was a better way.

How Husbands Feel About Forgiveness

Our husbands need and deserve our change of heart:

"When my wife makes a mistake and asks for my forgiveness, it's good for the asking. Why, when I make a mistake (and yes, I do fail her!), do I get the distinct impression that I am going to pay for that mistake for the rest of my life? Is this a 'girl thing' or what?"

"My thinking is when we get stuck in an unforgiving rut, willing to see only failures in our mate, we'll never be able to see the good in them. I would ask my wife, once she says she forgives me, to forgive me and move forward. Please don't stockpile it for future use and ignore the good I *am* doing!"

> *When your husband asks for your forgiveness, remember how freeing it feels to be forgiven without hesitation or reservation. Now do it!*

"Some of my failures have been doozies. Others are not even worth mentioning. But I swear my wife keeps a ledger somewhere. She remembers every mistake I've ever made. It's almost like she doesn't *want* to forget."

"If I could ask my wife just one thing regarding forgiveness it would be to let the incident go once we have worked through it. Please don't bring it up again and again, especially because I do try to not repeat the same mistake. When you do, my failure doesn't die—instead it takes on a life-form of its own."

Wiping the Slate Clean

Have you ever wondered just how many times your husband has forgiven you for those countless acts of carelessness you have committed? Some perhaps that left a sting on his otherwise stalwart heart? In my own case, the list goes on and on.

We have a choice when our husband fails us and seeks our forgiveness; we can walk in wisdom or bathe in bitterness. Honestly, most of our husband's failures aren't "fatal." Sometimes we wives have a tendency to overdramatize and turn our husband's failures into fatal flaws. And sometimes we seem to be recovering from amnesia! How is it that we have become so remarkably adept at suddenly remembering all the *wrong* things? The things we told our husband we had forgiven and forgotten eons ago?

Have we kept a ledger of all wrongdoings? If so, perhaps we have forgotten we can wipe it clean. Some would call this the purest form of love, for love keeps no record of wrongs, and pardon holds the power and hope for restoration and reconciliation. Bitterness, on the other hand, is poison. It is a slayer of souls.

Our husband needs to be forgiven for his transgressions, and he needs to know that we have forgotten them as well. We can change. We can forgive and we can forget. And, if we hold tight the lesson learned from Caroline, forgiving and forgetting make possible the miracle of falling in love all over again.

> *Remember, we are our children's greatest teachers. There is enormous truth to the adage that we reap what we sow. Show them by your example how to forgive and forget.*

Writing Your Legacy

How would you respond today if God placed the "pen of life" in your hand and asked you to write the rest of your life's story? Would you allow an unforgiving heart to determine the ending to your script? How will the ending to your story read?

Reflection

Forgiveness is an eternal gift. It is the gift that keeps on giving.

Finally, brothers, whatever is true, whatever is noble, whatever is right, whatever is pure, whatever is lovely, whatever is admirable—if anything is excellent or praiseworthy—think about such things.

—Philippians 4:8 NIV

Love breeds chivalry, and accepts nothing less. When we wait on the Lord, allowing Him to have control of our relationship lives, He leads us to His best for us. That is where chivalry lives.

—David W. Dickey,
network administrator

Chapter 10

Cherish His Chivalry

SOME SAY THE age of chivalry is past, that the spirit of romance is dead. The age of chivalry is never past, so long as there is a wrong left unredressed on earth," wrote British Anglican clergyman and writer Charles Kingsley.

Perhaps then, it is time to right one wrong left unredressed.

Forget the we're-technologically-superior-more-intelligent-and-more-independent self-talk we've been feeding ourselves for years. Being technologically superior to the generations before us doesn't erase our yearning for the mystery and magic of an old-fashioned love affair, does it?

Think about it: Hollywood certainly understands the feminine heart! They capitalize on the very notion that women will always be drawn to the "stuff" that fairy tales are made of. The idea that a man would proclaim his love for us, or wrestle to the finish to defend our honor, answers the age-old question inscribed on most every woman's heart: *Am I lovely enough to be protected, defended, and cherished by a man of honor—the man of my dreams?*

Warriors in Training

It was a glorious Friday afternoon in the fall of 1974, and my sophomore year of college. Working our way down the hall from philosophy class, we had just wrapped up a weeklong discussion of the current culture's values and customs. The class consisted of a colorful cast of characters. With the feminist movement in full swing, some of the young women were incensed that we were still considered the weaker gender. Using vivid descriptions, they expressed that anger. It was my first exposure to male bashing.

Undaunted, the professor asked the guys if they thought, given the strength of the women's movement, chivalry was still alive. Did the guys ever come to life! Never before had they been as vocal or participatory. Even the ballplayers who typically did more sleeping than speaking in class, found their voices that day.

The consensus? The guys were mystified by girls' misinterpretation of their well-intended acts of kindness. What was once called consideration was now called chauvinistic. Society, it seemed, was trying to persuade us that fathers and grandfathers completely missed the mark when they instilled in their sons and grandsons the ideal of treating a lady like a lady, with gentility and respect.

"Make up your minds, girls! What do ya'll want from us?" Paul, the captain of the baseball team vented—his Hollywood good looks highlighted by his deep Southern drawl. His band of brothers on the team echoed his frustration and uncertainty. And, with the ideology of chivalry left largely unsolved, class was dismissed.

Spilling into the corridor after class, continuing the conversation, a group of us soon reached the first of several double doors. Leslie and I paused while Paul held the door for us to pass through.

Take some time together with your husband and discuss your ideas of chivalry. Sometimes our ideas and expectations are different than our spouse's—thus disappointment sets in. Discuss where your ideas of chivalry originated and on what they are based.

With the overstated, fun-loving sense of style he was known for, Paul held the door with his right hand, and, tucking his left arm in at the waist, bowed, and said, "After you, ladies!"

Born out of our discussion, Leslie screamed at Paul, "Do you think I'm not capable of opening the door myself? Call it what you want, but I call it sexist! I do not need your help!" she ranted. Not surprisingly, Leslie's outburst drew an instant crowd.

Stripped of his dignity, Paul responded in the only way possible to save face amongst his peers. Thirty years later, his response holds as much impact for me today as it did then. In the best false bravado a nineteen-year-old guy could gather, Paul replied, "Which is exactly why I am holding it open for Judy. *She*," he overexaggerated, "is a lady!"

Without a doubt, it was Paul's chivalry, rather than my social graces, that elevated him past the point of retaliation. In fact, it provided him with the poise to protect the honor of that moment. How often have you seen a guy react to a situation with language and gestures that leave you feeling defiled? Fortunately, Paul did not succumb to anger. Because his character was stronger than his temper, his chivalry conveyed value, honor, and appreciation.

Discerning Our Divine Design

Paul's act of chivalry was a defining moment in my life, and I was so grateful God had created me to wear garments of gentility and grace. What an incredible calling! It was also my first glimpse into how a misguided feminist movement seemed determined to erase femininity and chivalry from the heart of history and its women. The same movement angrily opposed the belief that men were created to be gentlemen and protectors (warriors) dressed in breastplates of courage, integrity, and honor. A sense of knowing also "whispered" to me that the concept of chivalry would wither until, someday, a cry was heard to resurrect it to its rightful place in society.

> *For further reading on what it means to be a biblical woman today, Mary Farrar's* Choices: For Women Who Long to Discover Life's Best *(Sisters, Ore.: Multnomah, 1994) is highly recommended.*

Fast-forward to the year 2005. The notion that women were created to wear garments of gentility and grace has been further eradicated over the years. Many of us have struggled to some degree or another to be considered equal to or better than men in a world seen as unfair. Judging effectiveness by outcome would suggest the struggling may have been in vain. Many women are still frustrated and even more men are confused. However, in that pursuit of equality, have we unwittingly stripped our husband of his breastplate—his armor—of honor?

Driving the point home again, we *are* technologically superior to the generations before us. Surveys indicate women are more ambitious, more independent, and more intelligent than ever before. Yet how wise is it to attempt to thwart God's design for His own children? You and I should take caution not to let our blind ambition betray us.

Chelsea, a lovely young woman who is single, successful, and wise beyond her years, wonders if we have lost sight of who we are, who we were created to be, who men are, and who they were created to be. And, most importantly, who God is.

Part of the problem may be that we've grown disillusioned. In the humanness of life, our husband has disappointed us—which he will do again and again, just as we let him down. There will *always* be those "difficult" days in marriage. It doesn't mean we should cancel the original wedding covenant and create a new-and-improved version seemingly better suited for today's traditions. Though some try, they also fail. Marriage is sacred because God created its covenant. We cannot, with the mystery, magic, and wonder of God Himself, rewrite that which is written on the heart of mankind.

Is it possible that in our prideful quest to prove our we-can-do-anything-men-can-do point, we are trying to redesign what the Designer made our husband's heart to be?

The Joy of the Journey

Imagine planning a canoe trip on a river's rapids recognized the world over for their wonder and magnificence. But you're a pioneer at heart, always looking to forge ahead in new frontiers. You attempt to travel upstream—an inherent struggle against nature. You understand that when you set your course, and even though the current has *always* traveled in the same direction, you are determined to conquer the river! After all, you have what it takes. You're educated, clever, and well-prepared, and you know the river . . . or so you thought. Instead, your journey upriver is marked by frustration, untold challenges, and a stinging sense of failure. The joy of the journey, as it was intended, is lost on you. The wonder, thrill, and exquisite beauty are never to be discovered.

> *Men are great responders to positive encouragement. Show your husband that you are grateful for his chivalrous ways and wait to see how quickly he responds to your loving approval! (For the record, this "key" was submitted by one of the husbands who faithfully contributed to this book.)*

If you've been trying to travel upstream, won't you turn your "canoe" around? Doing so is not the mark of failure. Rather, it is the mark of intelligence and expresses your desire to experience the joy of the journey the way it was intended.

A Warrior's Tenderness

Most fascinating, the first man to respond to this topic of chivalry is still single. In fact, it is his quote that opens this chapter. Wisely waiting on "God's best" for his life and choice of a wife, the blessing of God's best may be close at hand. "I think chivalry is alive and well," this bright, young businessman shared, "living in the hearts and minds of those, whether young or old, who believe that people deserve to be treated with respect and kindness. Men should treat their wives (or the young lady who may become their wife) as God intended for us to treat them—with the love Jesus Christ had for the church."

While on a recent flight from Seattle to Memphis, Bob and I had the pleasure of meeting Bill, a captain flying for Northwest Airlines. The captain's demeanor—how he carried himself and treated those around him—convinced us he was a man of honor. Trusting that instinct, I approached and asked the married father of two teenagers if he might share his thoughts on chivalry. And so he did.

> *Do you remember Atticus Finch, the small-town Southern attorney who defends a man wrongly accused of a crime in the movie* To Kill a Mockingbird? *The instances of chivalry woven throughout the 1950s movie are beautiful. Atticus Finch leaves you with a wonderful model of what chivalry was, could be, and should be. Search through the movie archives to find some of those old movies about romance and honor that were made before Hollywood decided to leave little to the imagination.*

"As the head of our home, I am *called* to model chivalry. There's no need for me to create a new code for chivalry. That was created for us long ago in the Holy Bible. I simply try to line up my behavior with God's plan—His picture of chivalry. Likewise, in teaching my thirteen-year-old son what it 'looks like' to be a young man of honor, I again turn to the Bible. Because of our source, I must say he 'does it' better than most men.'"

Adding an exclamation point to his thoughts on chivalry, Bill shared his blessing for his bride on the "eve" of their twentieth wedding anniversary: "Deb, you are a gift from God. Our marriage means more to me than I ever could have imagined. I pray our marriage will continue to grow stronger, and our love for one another deepen each and every day, as I strive toward being the husband God wants me to be—the husband you deserve."

Telling It Like It Is

Elizabeth, an unmarried, thirty-two-year-old family physician believes, "Women are drawn to the beauty and magic of real romance because it is a longing *written* on our hearts by God. Society does their best to convince us those longings are the idealistic and silly notions of little girls and big-screen movie mania. Thus, we lock those dreams away in the back of our heart, never really believing our prince will come. The truth is God *has* created those men. We need to stop falling for the fallacies of society and step into God's love story, expecting greatness from His favored sons and valiant warriors." She goes on to share, "It breaks my heart when I see women, married and single alike, slapping the hands of God's sons as they reach out to protect and honor them."

Husbands have a similar yearning. It is to be that man of honor and a favored son. And while they are the first to admit they sometimes fall short of the mark, they also ask that we deal with them in grace when they fail us.

Spoken Like True Warriors

"My wife tries diligently to let me be the 'warrior.' The hard part is for her not to get wounded. I have to constantly remember the Lord tells me in His word that my wife is a gentle flower. Unfortunately, I sometimes charge in like a warrior. And I've learned it's very easy to bruise the rosebuds of a gentle flower . . ."

One husband and father of two laments about the misinterpretation that envelops chivalry today: "There are some who misunderstand the loving actions of a man who is genuine and full of chivalry.

In many respects I can't blame them. Men have abandoned their positions of warriors and become pirates and plunderers. When the 'knight' shows up, it's easy to assume this is the next ploy to thwart the defenses of women. Perhaps if men were more chivalrous, women would respect them more. And if women respected men more, they would be more chivalrous."

"Technology is one of the causes making chivalry more obsolete," added one family man. "For example, say with the invention of the remote car door openers, it is one less act—albeit a small one—that a gentleman can do for a lady as a sign of respect."

"I am proud—in a humble sort of way—to be the warrior, the gentleman, and to wear the 'armor' God has designed me to wear," offered a pastor, husband, and father of two. "But to whom much has been given, much will be required. I see my calling as a huge responsibility. So I am proud the Lord trusts me with his precious princess, though I also realize this means more than winning a 'trophy.' She is to be loved, nurtured, and returned to Him spotless and without blemish. That is what the Scriptures say is my duty, and I pray daily I can live up to it."

> *The Bible has beautiful and significant Scripture passages that exemplify God's idea of chivalry. For a glimpse into God's design of the heart of a warrior, look up these Scriptures: Proverbs 20:5; Romans 13:12; Ephesians 6:10–17; Philippians 1:27; and 1 Thessalonians 2:7. It is worth noting that according to this last verse, a man—even as a warrior—is called to have an attitude of tenderness. It is often eye-opening when we align a concept with God's Word.*

Turning Toward Truth

Yes, they will still stumble and fall. At times, as warriors, they will bruise "the rosebuds of a gentle flower." That is why, even in this age of superior technological advancements, they admit to turning to the Bible for guidance and discernment. What is written on their hearts needs to be nurtured with words of wisdom that are unfailing and eternal. Isaiah knew we would need that "constant" in our lives when he assured us: "the grass withers, the flower fades, but the word of our God stands forever" (Isa. 40:8).

History has also taught you and I the perils and perplexities of relying on ever-changing public opinions, myths, and ideologies. As far back as A.D. 67, Paul warns Timothy (and us!), "For the time will come when they will not endure sound doctrine; but wanting to have their ears tickled, they will accumulate for themselves teachers in accordance to their own desires, and will turn away their ears from the truth and will turn aside to myths" (2 Tim. 4:3–4).

It is evident the myths of feminism have made a mockery of marriage. Independence and power aren't the cure-all, as we once thought. Our pursuit of independence, equality, and power has failed us. It led us astray and, losing perspective of God's design of us, we made an even bigger mess of things. Putting power and pride aside and allowing our husband to model chivalry in our home, we learn that wisdom, strength, and confidence do not abandon us after all. By encouraging and expecting him to be the man he is called to be, we show our husband we are lovely and worthy of being cherished, protected, and defended. You see, for a man to be valiant, he must feel that a woman is vulnerable and in need of his gallantry. Only an incredibly strong woman understands how and when to offer her tender vulnerability.

Yes, "the age of chivalry is never past, so long as there is a wrong left unredressed on earth." We can't pretend we do not understand. You and I have heard the cry from the "empty places" of a man's heart. Husbands long for chivalry to be resurrected as the gift God intended it to be: true, noble, right, pure, lovely, admirable, and praiseworthy.

Sisters in Christ, God's gift to you is in the heart of the husband He chose for you—in the heart of the husband who longs to be the man of honor in your life. God's best for you is in the heart of your husband where *He* has written the love story. And with the mystery, magic, and wonder of God Himself—*that* is where chivalry lives.

———

Postscript: David Dickey, the wonderful young man whose quote opens this chapter, has just asked for our daughter's hand in marriage! (Bob knew in advance, as David first asked for his permission and blessing.) Preparing his proposal in the form of a PowerPoint presentation highlighting the blessings of biblical marriage, David knelt near Aubrey as she read it on his laptop. At the end of the presentation, red hearts popped up, followed by his marriage proposal. Taking just a few minutes to giggle, grin, jump on the couch, and twirl around the room, a normally reserved Aubrey *finally* responded with a resounding *"Yes!"* We look forward to adding David to the Carden clan in January 2006, when he and Aubrey begin their own covenant marriage.

Reflection

Chivalry is to romance as a star-studded sky is to the night: both are God's majestic handiwork—mysterious, miraculous, and magical.

My lover spoke and said to me,
  "Arise, my darling,
  my beautiful one, and come with me.
See! The winter is past;
  The rains are over and gone.
Flowers appear on the earth;
  the season of singing has come, . . ."

—Song of Songs 2:10–12 NIV

Grow old with me!
The best is yet to be,
The last of life, for which the first was made:
Our times are in His hand
Who saith "A whole I planned,
Youth shows but half; trust God:
See all, nor be afraid!

—Robert Browning

Chapter 11

Keep the Magic of Your Love Alive

THERE IS A picture I hold within the tender folds of my heart. One so beautiful only God could have painted it. My life here is nearly at an end. It is time for me to go to my heavenly reward. Lying in my bed many years from now, my white hair gently swept up into a bun, I beckon my beloved to come close. Bob takes my wisp of a hand into his weathered one and, sitting by my side, ever so gently asks, "What is it my dear?"

With my voice clear but eyes glistening with tears I say, ". . . the letter. Don't forget to read my special letter to you. Just open the lid to my hope chest. It's right there . . ."

Because God has yet to paint the rest of the picture, it is the only part of the "painting" I am able to share. But the letter is written, signed, sealed, and placed where Bob knows to find it. Tied with lavender ribbons, it is in my hope chest.

Not too long ago I shared the idea of the letter with an acquaintance. She was skeptical, reminding me of the possibility that our marriage *could* take a "wrong turn." "What if things don't turn out as you think they will? If you ask me, I'd wait to write the letter. You've bared your soul in a letter meant to be read in the future, based exclusively on faith," she cautioned me, shaking her head as she walked away.

Understanding the Covenant

She was right about my faith, but only partially. You see, I know Bob is the husband God chose for me. Because of that, God blesses our relationship and wants His best for our marriage. I also know my husband's character and commitment to not only me, but to our Father as well. The marriage covenant we made on the day of our wedding is not taken lightly by either of us. I know there is always the chance Bob

could hurt me deeply. However, I choose to put my faith in his character and in God's desire for a marriage that blesses us and brings Him
honor. Naturally, pain and disappointment are part of marriage—but
so is forgiveness, love, and restoration.

Allowing myself to love fully allows me to live fully. So the letter is written and placed in the hope chest. And should I go to my
heavenly reward before he does, Bob knows to read it. In fact, every
so often, I untie the beribboned letter and read it aloud. Reading the
words that tell the story of our love is more than magical: the words
seem to come alive! They make my soul sing and my heart dance with
delight. Reading the letter reminds me of the many reasons I love my
husband. And it reminds me that there is no greater power in this
world than the power of love.

You might say the letter is an insurance policy of sorts. By hang-
ing my heart out there on pure faith, I do not want to in any way
diminish the magic of our love. For it is not only my expectation of a
forever love, but God's as well. It is the reminder that because God
gave me *His* best when He blessed me with His favored son Bob, our
love deserves my best as well.

Isn't that what God expects from each of us? He blessed you and
me with our husbands. God knew in the beginning there would be
promises exchanged during a dreamy candlelit ceremony. He knew
that, because we were so crazy in love with our husband, the pledge to
love and honor him all the days of our life was a painless one to make.
He also knew that somewhere along the way—somewhere between
the marriage vows and mortgage payments, between the magical
and the mundane—we would discover that real love is learned in the
trenches of life. Yet, from disappointment to disappointment, tenderness to tenderness, and from joy to joy, love ultimately becomes its
own reward.

Along with the union of His beloved daughter and favored son,
He gave us another gift. He knew we would need direction and guidance, a how-to guide if you will, for it is also His desire that we keep
the magic of our love alive! If you think about it, it makes perfect sense
because, though everybody has an opinion, God has a plan. That plan
is for marriage to reflect the relationship spoken of in His Book.

Much is written on how to keep the magic of marriage alive.
You've probably tapped into many of those resources. But you're

always looking for more inspiration! Tonight, when all is still, sit down together with your husband and open the Bible. Even if you and your husband have wandered from the Word, run and find it. Dust it off. Set the popular periodicals aside. Ask yourselves: "Have we been looking for the magic in marriage on all the wrong pages?"

Collectively, we must be looking for the magic on all the wrong pages. Why else would the magic of so many marriages turn into misery? You know the old adage, "If you don't stand for something, you'll fall for anything." Have we been that naive, that ready and willing to accept what *sounds* like truth *as* truth? Often we mislead our own hearts by holding hard and fast to a false set of truths.

The *NIV Couples' Devotional Bible* (Zondervan, 1994) is an amazing source for the wisdom of God's Word and its practical application into our daily lives. Not only does it include a reading structure, but its themed devotions are designed to improve communication between a husband and wife. The applications and study helps in this Bible frequently add clarity on a topic within our marriage where confusion or chaos has taken hold.

In 1 Corinthians 13, Paul writes, "The greatest of these is love." Many of us implemented the famous "love chapter" into our wedding ceremony. We know the greatest of these is love. And in the context of marriage, we ask ourselves: *How do we keep the magic of our love alive?*

God Is in Relentless Pursuit of Our Hearts

Sisters in Christ, God is in passionate pursuit of your feminine heart. He is beckoning you to take this chance to write the rest of your love story. He wants you to love your husband as a favored son of His. Look at your husband through His eyes and heart. Commit or recommit your marriage to God. Consider renewing your marriage vows. The day Bob and I renewed our vows is forever etched on both our hearts. Take the sound wisdom you've gathered over the years, add it to your favorite Scriptures, and apply it to your marriage every day! It sounds almost too easy, but if it were, God would not be in such relentless pursuit of our hearts.

To love allows us to live fully. There's a great blurb floating around the Internet these days: "Life should not be a journey to the grave with the intention of arriving safely in an attractive and well-preserved body; but rather skid in sideways, champagne in one hand, chocolate in the other, body thoroughly used up, totally worn-out, and screaming, *'Woo hoo—what a ride!'"* While I'm not advocating you live a wild and reckless life, the blurb leaves you with the feeling that the author lived life to the utmost!

Do we forget to live life and experience marriage to the fullest? No wonder the magic dies. If we forget, we are guilty of the manslaughter of our own marriage! Do you want a rich relationship? Laugh with your husband. Have fun. Plan outings. Surprise him with an outrageous blessing! Bring your creative, romantic self back to life.

Tending the Tender Seedlings of Love

You've read the longings of your husband's heart. He longs for you to . . .

* Honor him, speaking respectfully of him to others. Allow him—no, *expect* him—to be the prince, rather than the pirate or plunderer.

* When he stumbles and falls, forgive him. Don't bury grudges deep within your heart. Love and forgiveness go hand in hand. They are the gifts that keep on giving.

* Make the bedroom of his heart a safe and sacred place where there is no greater miracle than that of love. The melody of that love is magical—so magical it still nearly takes his breath away.

* Be his friend and confidant. Encourage him to share the longings of his heart with you. Be a good listener. Take the treasures he shares with you and hold them close to your heart.

* Stay lovely for him. He's an incredibly visual creature—it's important to him. He's proud of you, his bride!

* Encourage him to nurture strong friendships with his brothers or friends, allowing him to unwind and download during his downtime away from home. Don't make his downtime conditional on how much downtime you have. At the end of the day, it all works out. And remember, he will be thrilled to see you once he returns!

* Work through any issues of jealousy. Trudging through life wearing brokenhearted shoes is a surefire way to replace magic with absolute misery.

* Lift God's favored son, your husband, in prayer. Pray fearlessly, fervently, and unceasingly. Pray silently, pray out loud, pray together, pray Scriptures, pray spontaneously—but pray!

A Personal Excerpt

Even if you're not quite ready to share it with your husband, would you consider writing a love letter to him? Will you boldly proclaim that love, perhaps based on pure faith, and write the words to your love story? Whether you've been married five months or fifty-five years, trust that God, the author of your love story, will guide you to "walk out" the rest of the story.

Writing that letter *is* an act of faith—one I've made and am glad I did. Below is a brief excerpt from that letter. It's also my assurance of accountability. Many will read this excerpt and many will hold me accountable. I ask that you, too, hold me accountable, and I gratefully accept the responsibility.

Dear Bob,

By the time you read this letter, the angels will have carried me home. But I wanted you to have this written legacy with the words to our love story. Thank you for being a man of honor—a man always after God's heart. Throughout the years, your character and commitment were one of life's greatest constants. Your loving me made all the difference in my life and the children's as well. It stirred my heart and soothed my soul. It helped quiet the storms of life. It gave me the courage to reach for the stars, with you boosting me up each time so that I might touch them.

Ne'er a moment will pass—even in heaven's time—when I won't be thinking of you. Your face—with the look of love it has for a lifetime shown me—will forever flash throughout the hollows of my heart. Surely we sang the sonnets of each other's soul long before the sound of our heartbeats were even audible. Could it be my beloved that we danced in each other's dreams long before we were even born? Folks say our love is magical. It is that . . . and more. It is magical, marvelous, and miraculous. And I believe the legacy of our love will live on for generations to come.

Remember, my beloved . . . with each whisper of the wind, you'll hear the swoosh of the wings of the angels I've asked to watch over you. And until we meet again, know that only God has loved you more than I.

———

The rest of the story . . .

That's how much faith I have in our marriage of three . . . in God, Bob, and me. I am not a "Pollyanna," refusing to look at the harsh realities of life. I will always experience disappointment, disillusionment, and pain. But I will try my best not to let it cloud what I know is God's best for our marriage. Nor will I sleepwalk through life. Instead, I choose to live out my marriage as God intended when He united me with His favored son: with every ounce of miracle, mystery, and magic I can muster!

Even on the days when my heart gets bruised or I want to throw up my hands in exasperation, I marvel as God reveals His gift of love in our marriage. As each moment of our journey is unfurled, I am reminded there is no mystery . . . no miracle . . . no wonder greater than love and marriage.

Each of us has those moments that seem to beg forgiveness and promise change. It's what we do with them that counts. Perhaps you have experienced one of those moments while reading this book. You know the time has come for you to turn your heart back toward home. Some women have wandered farther than others. But truth has tickled each of us, telling us it is time to look upon our husband as our greatest treasure. We are armed not only with the desire for a richer marriage, but with the spiritual insight found in the Word of God!

I pray that your marriage be reignited with a love so deep, you and your husband will stand in awe of what God has done. Be prepared *to* change and *for* change. Even if you have approached this journey feeling a little weak-kneed, remember you have nothing to lose and everything to gain. God is beckoning you to draw close . . . so that He might inscribe the second half of your love story onto the pages of your heart.

Reflection

When the winter of your life is nearly passed and you want to relive the mystery, miracle, and magic of a marriage well lived, your heart need only rewind to the reel entitled, "Once upon our love story."

Sources

Arp, David and Claudia. *The Second Half of Marriage: Facing the Eight Challenges of Every Long-Term Marriage.* Grand Rapids: Zondervan, 1998.

Browning, Robert. "Rabbi Ben Ezra."

Burns, Robert. "A Red, Red Rose."

Christenson, Evelyn. *What Happens When Women Pray.* Wheaton, Ill.: Victor Books, 1992.

Eldredge, John. *Wild at Heart.* Nashville: Nelson, 2001.

Farrar, Mary. *Choices: For Women Who Long to Discover Life's Best.* Sisters, Ore.: Multnomah, 1994.

Gray, John. *Men Are from Mars, Women Are from Venus.* New York: HarperCollins, 1992.

Leman, Kevin. *Sheet Music: Uncovering the Secrets of Sexual Intimacy in Marriage.* Wheaton, Ill.: Tyndale House, 2003.

Morley, Patrick. *What Husbands Wish Their Wives Knew About Men.* Grand Rapids: Zondervan, 1998.

Roop, Shay. *For Women Only: God's Design for Female Sexuality and Intimacy.* Chattanooga, Tenn.: AMG Publishers, 2004.

Spiegelberg, Nancy. "If Only I Had Known You." © 1974. Used by permission of the author.